From
HORROR
to
HOPE

D0401969

From
HORROR
to
HOPE

DAVID & BETH GRANT
with
JONATHAN & JENNIFER BARRATT

CHARISMA
HOUSE

Most Charisma Media products are available at special quantity discounts for bulk purchase for sales promotions, premiums, fund-raising, and educational needs. For details, call us at (407) 333-0600 or visit our website at www.charismamedia.com.

FROM HORROR TO HOPE by David and Beth Grant with Jonathan and Jennifer Barratt
Published by Charisma House, an imprint of Charisma Media
600 Rinehart Road, Lake Mary, Florida 32746

This book or parts thereof may not be reproduced in any form, stored in a retrieval system, or transmitted in any form by any means—electronic, mechanical, photocopy, recording, or otherwise—without prior written permission of the publisher, except as provided by United States of America copyright law.

Unless otherwise noted, all Scripture quotations are taken from the Holy Bible, New International Version®, NIV®. Copyright © 1973, 1978, 1984, 2011 by Biblica, Inc.® Used by permission of Zondervan. All rights reserved worldwide. www.zondervan.com. The "NIV" and "New International Version" are trademarks registered in the United States Patent and Trademark Office by Biblica, Inc.®

Scripture quotations marked AMP are from the Amplified® Bible (AMP), Copyright © 2015 by The Lockman Foundation. Used by permission. www.Lockman.org.

Scripture quotations marked ESV are from the Holy Bible, English Standard Version. Copyright © 2001 by Crossway Bibles, a division of Good News Publishers. Used by permission.

Scripture quotations marked KJV are from the King James Version of the Bible.

Scripture quotations marked NKJV are taken from the New King James Version®. Copyright © 1982 by Thomas Nelson. Used by permission. All rights reserved.

Copyright © 2022 by Project Rescue Foundation
All rights reserved

Visit the authors' website at www.projectrescue.com.

Cataloging-in-Publication Data is on file with the Library of Congress.
International Standard Book Number: 978-1-63641-148-4
E-book ISBN: 978-1-63641-149-1

Some names and identifying details have been changed to protect the privacy of those individuals.

While the author has made every effort to provide accurate internet addresses at the time of publication, neither the publisher nor the author assumes any responsibility for errors or for changes that occur after publication. Further, the publisher does not have any control over and does not assume any responsibility for author or third-party websites or their content.

22 23 24 25 26 — 9 8 7 6 5 4 3 2 1
Printed in the United States of America

This book is dedicated to our faithful God, the ultimate Rescuer, Redeemer, and Restorer. For twenty-five years we've been amazed by His power to replace the horror of sexual slavery with hope, healing, and heaven.

"Come and see what God has done."
—PSALM 66:5

CONTENTS

PREFACE

A SEQUEL TO *Beyond the Soiled Curtain* has begged to be written for more than ten years. Now the time has come. What began in South Asia as an outreach to trafficked and sexually exploited women has grown into an international ministry reaching more than fifty thousand women and children each year. Now we celebrate twenty-five years since the birth of Project Rescue in the red-light districts of South Asia.

Tragically, sex trafficking and sexual exploitation have continued to explode in our world. But as more courageous colleagues on several continents have responded to the needs of victims, Project Rescue's network has grown in unexpected ways and places. Time and again, through miracles great and small, we've been reminded that rescuing and restoring women and children who've been sexually exploited is in the very heart and mission of God.

The following pages contain stories of women and children whose lives have been transformed from the unimaginable horror of this injustice. It is also the story of a growing network of Project Rescue ministry leaders with their own stories who continue to battle this evil relentlessly. They are passionate and professional, caring and dedicated so that victims of sexual exploitation can experience freedom, healing, and empowerment as children of God.

From Horror to Hope is dedicated to the courageous Project Rescue ministry pioneers—past and present—who have personally taken destiny-changing hope to thousands of the world's most vulnerable women and children in the darkest streets of our world:

Ambika	South Asia
April and Jerry Foster	Antwerp, Belgium
Brianna Petersen	South Asia
Cindy and Travis Mikeal	Finland
Devaraj	South Asia
Easo and Leela	South Asia
Eddi	South Asia
Fiona Bellshaw	Spain
Ivan and Sheila Satyavrata	South Asia
Joni Middleton	France
Joy Krajcek	France
Kevin and Lucy Donaldson	South Asia
Lisa Russi	South Asia, France
Maile	South Asia
Mark and Cathy Daniels	South Asia

Mathew and Suha	South Asia
Mrinalini	South Asia
Nancy Raatz	Moldova
Raegan Glugosh	Europe
Rajnish and Orina	South Asia
Rebecca	South Asia
Vinita	South Asia

Because of the priority given to protecting ministry leaders, local ministries, and the women and children they serve, full names and locations are not disclosed, and some names have been changed.

The stories you are about to read are their stories, made possible by their faith, sacrifice, and compassion. They are the real heroes of the Project Rescue story. It has been our privilege to serve with them for the last twenty-five years. They have inspired us to believe God for freedom for the women and children held captive in sex slavery.

Chapter 1

JOURNEY TO THE FRONT PORCH OF HELL

TINA WAS A beautiful, happy, vibrant girl living with her two brothers and sister in a little village outside Kathmandu, Nepal. Her dark eyes danced when she smiled. Tina constantly pushed her long, shiny black hair out of those eyes. Every morning she awoke to see the towering peaks of the Himalayas in the distance. It was a beautiful place. Tina's family was poor, though she did not know it. They had enough to eat, and her family loved her.

One day when Tina was just a few months shy of nine years old, a man came to their home and spoke in quiet tones with her father. Her father brought her into their one-room shack and introduced her to the man. "This is Raju. You will be going with him to a beautiful city far, far away to work in a rich lady's house," her father explained. The family would send her to school and take care of her. All she needed to do was go with the man and do everything he told her. Tina loved to wander through the streets of her village and even to the hills beyond. Sometimes she lost track of time and got in trouble with her mother. Mama said to her in a strict tone, "Tina, you cannot wander off. You must listen to this man." The man smiled a crooked smile and told Tina she was pretty and that the people were going to love her.

It seemed like a dream. Tina had never been outside her city, never been inside a school or even ridden a bus. Now she would go to this beautiful place and have a magical life. She never imagined such a thing would happen to her. She was sad and cried a little, but Mama gently wiped away her tears and said everything would be wonderful. Tina would make new friends and be educated. Mama and Papa kissed Tina and said goodbye. Her brothers and sister hugged her as well.

The man was nice. They went to the bus station in the village and took the bus to Kathmandu. The bus was very crowded. Some people stood in the aisles. One man brought a goat. Some boys rode on the top of the bus with the luggage. It was a lot to take in. The bus made funny noises that Tina had never heard before, a kind of growling sound from time to time. A pipe at the back of the bus belched black smoke. The smell made Tina a little upset in her stomach.

Tina pressed her face against the window. The hills rolled by so fast. The bus arrived in Kathmandu in less than an hour. The city was amazing—so many people, and all the big buildings. It was unlike anything she had ever seen.

The bus stopped at the train station, and she and Raju got off the bus and went inside. They walked up to the ticket window, and Raju bought two tickets for a city in South Asia. They did not have to wait long. The train was also very crowded.

The trip was long—two full days. As the train descended from the hill country of Nepal to the plains of North India, it started to get hot and dusty. Tina had never been hot before. The summers in her village were warm. She liked that, but this! The man began to sweat. He took out a filthy handkerchief and wiped his brow.

When it got dark, Tina leaned against Raju's shoulder and went to sleep. When she woke after the second night, the bus came into a very strange place. It was nothing like home. The streets were crowded with people. The air hung thick with the smell of exhaust. Tina asked where they were. Raju told her, "This is your new home." Tina had never heard of this place. Could this be the magical place Raju spoke about?

Tina's new home was a sprawling city of stunning architecture and lush parks. Since independence, it had become the commercial center of the nation, with soaring skyscrapers ringing its harbor. Millions of people had migrated there in search of a better life, and many of them had joined its middle class by graduating from one of the city's universities or succeeding in business.

This was not the city Tina would come to know. There is another city within this city—one that is darker, foreboding, and sinister. It can be found in hundreds of thousands of shacks in sprawling slums where millions dream of a better life but seem shut out of it. This is like the city portrayed in the commercial film *Slumdog Millionaire*, the story of a young man whose dream is fulfilled when he becomes a contestant on a TV game show. For most of the men, women, and children living in the city's slums, there are no game shows, just grinding poverty and the hopelessness born of believing there is no way out. It looks like a sepia print of browns and blacks and shadows. It was not like her village in the hills of Nepal. It did not feel good.

Finally, the train pulled into the station, where Raju ordered a taxi. After a few minutes, Tina sensed that they were not going to a magical place. As the taxi traveled deeper into the dark underbelly of the city, she felt herself shiver. She asked Raju where they were going. He told her not to worry; everything would be fine.

After more than an hour they rode into a place with a lot of men in the street. They got out of the taxi and walked down a narrow alley. They arrived at a house with a dirty curtain hanging in the door. An old woman leaned against the doorpost. She did not look nice. Surely this was not the rich lady.

"Where is the maharani?" Raju inquired of the old woman.

"The maharani is holding court inside the palace," the old woman flatly intoned as she pointed down a dark hallway with a flickering fluorescent light.

As Raju and Tina walked down the hall, she saw little rooms, no more than three feet by six feet, each with tattered cloths hanging haphazardly from crooked curtain rods. She could hear strange noises from some of the rooms. This could not be the rich lady's house that her papa had spoken of.

After what seemed like the longest walk of her life, Raju and Tina came into a kitchen. Four women about her mama's age sat there. None of them smiled. Their eyes seemed dead. Two of them smoked.

"This is the new one?" the oldest woman asked.

"Yes, this is the new one," Raju replied.

"She's a little skinny, but she'll do," the woman said with no emotion. The woman looked at her as if she were a goat. "I'll give you 5,000 rupees [about $140] plus the bus fare."

"Five thousand rupees? You old thief! She is easily worth 7,000," Raju replied with indignation.

The old woman held her ground. "Five thousand rupees, take it or leave it."

Raju took the money and walked out without saying a word. The smile was gone; the warmth was gone.

The old woman took Tina by the hand and walked her into one of the cubicles. "A man is coming to see you," she said with a hard edge in her voice. "You do what he tells you."

Two minutes later a man came in. He wasn't old or

young. He was neither handsome nor ugly. A greasy shock of hair hung down over his forehead. His breath was terrible. He told Tina she was pretty and that he liked her. Then he did things she knew nothing about. It hurt. It hurt so much. Tina screamed, "You are hurting me!" The man started acting crazy. He clamped his hand around Tina's throat and hurt her more. She felt like her belly was on fire. She shook and cried. It was the worst thing that had ever happened to her.

The man finished and left. Tina curled up into a ball and cried quietly. "What is this? What is happening to me?" After some minutes, another man pulled back the curtain and entered the cubicle. He was drunk and smelled terrible. Tina cried out, "No! No! Please no."

The old woman came into the room and slapped Tina across the face. "Shut up, you brat! Do what you're told." Tina thought her head would explode. Her mama had spanked her, but no one had ever treated her like this. She was dazed and confused. The man came back. And so did others—eight that first night.

Tina did not know it, but she had just entered a hell of abuse and torture that would continue throughout her young life. Every day the same routine. Sometimes up to ten men in a night. She asked the old woman about the rich lady and the nice house. The old woman threw her head back and laughed scornfully. "Rich lady? Nice house? I'm your rich lady, girl. I am your maharani."

Something inside Tina began to die. Hope. Love. The light in her beautiful black eyes slowly went out. By her ninth birthday, it was gone. Her eyes were dead. Tina's life became nothing but the attempt to survive one more day. When Tina was thirteen, she became pregnant. The old woman let her keep the baby. When her baby was born, he was so beautiful, with his little round cheeks. Tina decided to name him after Lord Krishna, which means "the all-attractive one." Each morning as the sun began to rise and the men went home, she would lie on the bed in her cubicle and hold little Krishna close. He was the only good thing in her world. She prayed that he would not have to live in this hell.

ELENA

The dull thud of artillery shells grew closer and closer. Elena's mother told her it was time to leave. Elena's family had been watching the news on Channel One in their city of Horlivka. Every day the Russian soldiers got closer to their home. "We can't stay, Elena," her mother told her. "You know about the Russians. They do terrible things." Every Ukrainian had grown up on stories about the Muskali, the slang term Ukrainians used to describe the Russians. The fall of communism in the 1990s had ended three hundred years of Russian rule and caused Ukrainians to hope for a better life, a life like the Poles and Czechs had found after gaining their freedom from the Russians. Elena's babushka (grandmother) told of Russian atrocities when the Red Army soldiers "liberated" them during the Second World War. They raped the women and killed most of the men, except for the local criminals they left in charge as the Red Army marched west to Berlin.

There was no time. They threw a few clothes into two suitcases and ran down the stairs of their flat. It was just the two of them. Elena never knew her father. Her mother told her that he loved vodka more than her, and she had kicked him out when Elena was just a baby. For all her sixteen years, it had been Elena and her mama. They were best friends—well, at least most of the time. Mama was an English teacher in the public school. She was beautiful and smart. Elena wanted to be just like her—to go to the linguistic university in Kyiv as her mother had and earn her baccalaureate degree and then a master's. Perhaps she would live in Kyiv and own her own apartment. Or maybe she would move to the Czech Republic or Germany. One day Elena would marry a handsome boy, have two children, and have a happy family. Like most Ukrainian girls, her dreams usually went to family.

Elena and her mother made it to a camp west of Slavyansk, about fifty miles north of their home, a trip they could have easily made in an hour and a half by car. In a war zone, it took two days. Elena and her mother were exhausted by the trip. But at least they were safe. The camp was jammed with more than a thousand people like Elena and her mom. They were assigned a tent with two other families. It wasn't too bad. The food was awful, but at least it was hot.

The camp was filled with all kinds of people, some good and some not so good. Elena's mama told her to be careful. She tried to be. Ukrainian girls learn to be careful: to look to the side when they walk down the street, not to make eye contact with people they do not know, and not to talk to strange men, especially foreign men. Not that many foreign men came to Horlivka, so they were not hard to spot. The Americans wore jeans and sneakers and smiled all the time. To her the smiling was strange. "Why do they smile at people they don't know?" Elena wondered.

A few weeks after arriving in the camp, Elena noticed a boy, a very good-looking boy—tall and blond. She thought him to be about nineteen or twenty. At first he would just wave and smile. One day he made a joke as Elena was standing with her hands on her hips.

"You know, a man went to his house, and his wife was standing in the door with her hands on her hips. She began to speak to him in an angry voice. He said, 'Woman, if my cap is tilted to the right side of my head, you cannot speak. If it is tilted to the left, you cannot speak. If it is on the back of my head, you may speak.' The woman looked at him and said, 'You old fool. If my hands are on my hips, I don't care how you wear that stupid cap.'"

Elena laughed. The boy was funny. "May I speak?" he asked.

Elena laughed again. "You may," she replied, taking her hands off her hips.

"I'm Andriy," he said pleasantly. "What is your name, princess?"

"My name is Elena."

"Ah, the czaritza, Elena."

Elena laughed again. She liked Andriy. He was so cute.

They walked a little way together. Elena realized she had been gone awhile. "I'd better go," Elena said brightly.

"Goodbye, princess."

Elena glowed the rest of the day. It was the first time she had been happy since they fled their home. Mama asked where she had been. "Oh, nowhere," Elena responded.

"Does nowhere have a name?"

"No, no name," Elena replied evasively.

Elena saw Andriy every day for a week. They walked. They drank tea at the little kiosk inside the camp. He told silly jokes. Elena was in love. Then one evening, just as the sun was going down, Andriy pulled Elena close and kissed her. She had kissed other boys, but nothing like this. Andriy asked Elena if she could come out later and walk. She waited until her mother fell asleep, and she quietly slipped on her tennis shoes and went to the place she had arranged to meet Andriy. She did not see the man who quietly came up behind her. She felt a hand on her mouth and heard a hoarse voice she did not recognize whisper: "Be very quiet, princess, if you want to stay healthy."

Elena was terrified. Her legs began to shake. She wanted to scream but knew she dare not. They walked to a dark place at the edge of the camp and went out. The man pushed her into the trunk of a car where she stayed for two days. Elena began to sob. She had heard of such things but never knew anyone who was taken. The car stopped from time to time. The man opened the trunk and then told Elena to get out. The man gave her a stale ham and cheese sandwich. Then he shoved her into the trunk of his car again. The man knew all the back roads between Ukraine and their destination, Antwerp, Belgium, desolate back roads with no lights and no border crossings. Whatever a Europe of open borders meant to the business leaders in Brussels, Berlin, and Paris, Europe had become a trafficker's heaven—no border crossings between countries, no nosey border guards, an almost straight shot from Slavyansk to the cities of Western Europe. After two days of hard driving, they reached their destination, a drab apartment in a working-class neighborhood of Antwerp.

Elena was exhausted as she stumbled up the steps to the back entrance to the apartment building. Her mind was foggy from sleeplessness and hunger. The man pulled her up the steps to a fourth-floor landing. "Here you go, princess, your new home," he said with a sneer.

He rang the bell, and a woman who was about

twenty-five slowly opened the door. "Oleg? Is this the new one?"

"Yeah, Tatiana; this is the princess," the man said wearily.

They walked down a hallway to a living room where a dozen other Ukrainian and Russian girls stared idly into space. Some of them were drugged. Others languidly drew on cigarettes. The room was thick with stale smoke.

Tatiana motioned to a large couch. "Sit," she commanded Elena. Elena half stumbled onto the couch. She leaned her head back and closed her eyes. She began to drift off when a hand grabbed her shoulder and shook her roughly.

It was another man, about thirty-five or forty. His tone, like his face, was hard and mean.

"So, missy, you belong to me now, understand? You are a working girl, and you have to start earning your keep." Elena had entered the netherworld of sex trafficking. This would be her world. She would never see her mother again.

ADANNA

Adanna grew up in the Nigerian town of Benin City. She was the second child of her father's third wife, as polygamy was common practice in Nigeria. Her father never seemed very interested in Adanna, even though her name meant "her father's daughter." He gave most of his attention to the son of his first wife. She sat at the end of the dinner table far from her father. She could not have been farther away if she had been on the moon. When he spoke to her at all, his tone was no different than when he spoke to a taxi driver. Her mother was just sixteen when she married her father. Mommy was now thirty-five but still very pretty. The first wife hated her and her children. When her father was away, the first wife would scream obscenities at Adanna's mother. Sometimes she slapped her.

Adanna's mother went to a Pentecostal church near her home. The pastor was called Prophet Ezekiel, and like so many Nigerian preachers, he thundered when he preached. He constantly preached on giving to the ministry and told them that giving would break the bondages off their lives. He often spoke of visions and dreams God gave him. Adanna always marched to the front of the church as the choir swayed to the African praise music and put four hundred or five hundred Nigerian naira (roughly equivalent to one US dollar) in the offering bucket. The prophet would nod his head and smile approvingly.

When Adanna turned eighteen, her father called her to him one night after dinner.

"Adanna, I have made arrangements for you to go to Madrid. You will be a nanny for a white family."

Adanna knew girls who had gone to Europe to be nannies or dancers, or to clean the white people's houses. It seemed like a good possibility. There weren't many job opportunities in Benin City. More than 60 percent of Nigeria's exploding population is under the age of twenty-five, which means there aren't many jobs for young people. Even university graduates find jobs only half the time. Many of the best and brightest Nigerian youth leave the country for Europe or America. Adanna knew one man who waited seventeen years to obtain a visa to go to the United States. So the chance to leave seemed like an answer to prayer.

Her father looked at her sternly. "Adanna, nothing is free in this world. You must pay back every naira to the people who sponsor you. And you must obey them."

"Yes, Daddy," Adanna replied. Even though she had never felt close to her father, she respected him.

"How much will my debt be, sir?"

"More than 50,000 euros [roughly $55,000]," her father said.

Adanna had no idea what a euro was or how much she would be paid. A boy at church once told her that the streets in Europe were paved with gold, that everyone in Europe was rich, and that even the Africans became rich. Adanna also had no idea that the procurer had paid her father €1,000 euros or that many families in her city had found selling their daughters a great way to make money. Adanna knew none of this.

She was excited to go, excited to see a new country, excited to become prosperous. Over the next few weeks, Adanna prepared to leave. She packed her clothes into a suitcase her mother bought for her in the bazaar.

The night before Adanna was to begin her journey, her mother told her they were having a special anointing service at the church for her and three other girls headed for Spain. They met in a back room behind the sanctuary. Prophet Ezekiel swept through the door in a long white robe with a crucifix hanging around his neck. The women of the church formed a circle around Adanna and the other three girls. They began to sing and speak in tongues. For more than an hour they sang. Then Prophet Ezekiel said, "Do you feel the power?" He punched the word *power*.

"God is coming upon you." The prophet drew out the word *God* into two emphatic syllables. He took a bottle of oil and anointed each girl by pouring it on her head. He took the crucifix and touched their foreheads. He then began to cast out the spirit of snake and broke the curses on them. Several of the girls fell to the floor, writhing and screaming. The wailing women pressed in and pumped their arms in a chopping motion to break Satan's power. One of the girls vomited. The ceremony was a mix of Christianity and tribal religion that prevails in many of the independent African churches. To Westerners, it smacks of voodoo rituals in Haiti. To many Africans, it is simply part of their religious universe, as normal as prayer and worship.

Once the demons had been cast out, Prophet Ezekiel looked at the girls and admonished them, "You must obey the people who bring you to Spain. You must do everything they tell you. You must pay back your debts."

Adanna did not know it, but Prophet Ezekiel also received a "blessing" from the procurer. He too was part of a vast web of relationships that made sex trafficking in Africa possible.

The ceremony ended. The ladies of the church hugged and kissed Adanna and told her they would be praying for her. When Adanna got home, she fell into bed, exhausted by the ceremony. She was asleep in minutes.

Early the next morning, Adanna's mama woke her and told her that she needed to dress quickly. It was almost time to go. Adanna pulled herself out of bed, still a little groggy from the night before.

A man met Adanna and her mother at the bus station. He was not a handsome young man, but he was not unpleasant either. Like them, he was a Yoruba, tall and lean. He had a face she had seen on hundreds of boys his age. He smiled kindly to Adanna's mother and politely introduced himself. "I am Benjamin; I will be your daughter's escort to Spain."

Benjamin told Adanna's mother that he would take good care of her daughter. It was time to go. Adanna's mother gave her a hug and kissed her softly. Adanna felt her mother's tears on her cheeks. Adanna also began to cry. Mama reached up and brushed Adanna's tears.

"Goodbye, my sweet girl. Make us proud. Work hard. And remember, you must obey."

"Yes, Mommy. I will do everything they tell me to do."

Adanna's mother gave her a plastic bag with snacks for the journey, some biscuits and samosas (meat-filled African pastries).

When Adanna sat in her seat, the young man handed her a passport. It was a fake. Her school photo had been pasted into the folder. Her new name would be Matilda Kwame. Adanna didn't think much about it. It was not uncommon for people to buy fake IDs and pay bribes. In some countries, the people may pay as many as sixteen bribes every month. It is just the way things are.

The bus made its way from Benin City to Lagos, then to Niger and on through the desert regions of Libya. After three weeks, the bus arrived in the Tunisian capital of Tunis. Adanna talked to other girls on the bus. Some were headed to Spain, others to Milan. All told, ten girls in the bus were going to work in Europe. They were all girls like her, most of them from Benin City. They shared their excitement and giggled together and dreamed of their new lives in Europe. Though none of them were aware of it, they were on a modern caravan route carved out by sex traffickers to export young girls from Africa to Europe.

The flight to Madrid took just two and a half hours, nothing like the bus trip. Getting through passport control took just a few minutes. Adanna asked, "Will we be going straight to the people's house?"

"Oh no," the boy replied. "First we must take you to our hostel, where you can shower, rest, and get your new clothes. We will meet the people tomorrow." They drove to a "hostel," where she saw other girls her age, all from Nigeria, most from her hometown of Benin City.

The next afternoon, Benjamin took Adanna to a nice suburb of Madrid. Adanna looked out the window of the taxi the entire trip. Madrid was so clean, nothing like Africa with its dust, heat, and humidity. There was no garbage in the streets, no buses belching oily black exhaust. Adanna felt blessed.

The ride took about forty-five minutes. They pulled up in front of a beautiful, three-story house. "These people must be so rich," Adanna mused. "I will be working for a rich family."

A beautiful woman answered the door and introduced herself as Señora Valdez. Adanna smiled at her. Even during the day, the woman looked very smart. Her hair and makeup were perfect. Long gold earrings gave the impression of elegance and poise. It was hard to tell how old she was. Adanna could never tell how old white people were. This one had small crow's feet accentuating her large green eyes. Adanna had never seen anyone with green eyes before. They were beautiful.

"Welcome, Adanna. Welcome to our home," the woman said pleasantly. "We are happy you have come."

Señora Valdez showed Adanna to her room. It was a small room behind the laundry room but larger than her room at home. It was clean and nice, painted in light yellow.

After putting her bag down on the bed, Adanna and Señora Valdez went to the kitchen, where they sat down at a pretty table with fresh flowers in the middle. Adanna had never seen anything like this in Nigeria.

"Now, Adanna, your job will be to clean our house every day. I will give you a schedule of what is to be done every day and every week," Señora Valdez said in a calm, even tone. "It is most important that you do everything exactly as I tell you."

It was a good day. Señora Valdez was elegant and gracious, with an old-world charm that was a mark of the Spanish upper class but was completely new to Adanna. She met the cook and the driver, both of whom referred to Señora Valdez as "Doña," which she was told was a term of respect that working-class people used when addressing members of the upper class. Adanna thought she would try it. When Adanna next saw Señora Valdez, she addressed her as "Doña." Señora Valdez was pleased. "Smart girl," she replied.

Later that afternoon, the Valdez children came home from school. The girl, who was about fourteen, looked like a younger version of Doña Valdez. The boy was about eleven. Even though Adanna just met him, she could see he was a clown, the light in his mother's eye.

Señor Valdez was in Geneva on a business trip. He did not return for several days. When he walked through the door, Adanna was dusting furniture in the living room.

"Arturo, meet our new maid," Señora Valdez said. "This is Adanna."

"It is nice to meet you, Adanna," Señor Valdez replied in a refined tone.

Señor Valdez was tall, handsome, and, like the Doña, elegant. He held his head at an angle that suggested centuries of breeding and power. This was a strong, proud man, a respected man. His father, Adanna later learned, had served in the Cortes Generales, the Spanish parliament. His grandfather had been a member of the Cabinet. The servants called him "Don." Adanna felt her prayers were being answered.

Adanna never had a conversation with Señor Valdez, but he was always pleasant and kind. Adanna liked the Valdezes. They gave her Sundays off. She found a Nigerian church near the center of the city. Everything was going well.

Until it wasn't.

One beautiful summer weekend, the Doña and the children were away visiting her family in Galicia. They would be gone for a week.

August in Madrid is hot, but not like Nigeria. Europe was never as hot as Nigeria. It was, however, unseasonably warm with temperatures soaring into the upper nineties. The air conditioner never stopped. Adanna went to sleep one night, dreaming the dreams that young girls dream.

She wasn't asleep long when something awakened

her. It was a soft kiss on her neck. As she turned to look, there was Don Valdez, dressed in silver silk pajamas. He smiled slightly and said, "Adanna, I have been watching you. You are beautiful, and I am so glad you are here." He kissed her again, this time on the mouth.

Adanna was a little scared but also flattered. Don Valdez was so handsome, like a movie star in the old movies she enjoyed so much.

Adanna kissed him back. Before she knew it, she and Don Valdez were intimate. It did not seem wrong. Her own father had four wives. She was also fairly sure that he had girlfriends. She looked into Don Valdez's eyes and felt love.

Don Valdez came to her every night during that week. It was wonderful. Don Valdez was wonderful. When Doña came home, nothing changed. Don Valdez was his charming self, gracious and kind. Things went on as they had. Life was good.

Until it wasn't.

One night when Doña and the children were gone, Don Valdez came to Adanna. This time was different. Don Valdez had been drinking. His personality was changed. He said and did things that he had never said and done before. He was aggressive. The night left Adanna feeling hurt and alone. For the first time, she was ashamed. She cried into her pillow.

The next day Adanna did not see Don Valdez. She hoped she would not. But she remembered the words of her father and Prophet Ezekiel: "You must obey. You must do everything they tell you." She thought of the indignities her own mother endured at the hands of the first wife. She was in Spain by herself—no money, no connections, and a fake passport. Adanna was powerless. She had to get by.

Don Valdez came to her more frequently. Sometimes he was as sweet as he had ever been, but those other times... Adanna could not bear to think of those times. It seemed like hell. It was strange. The house was so beautiful, the family so nice. Sometimes hell seems like a nice place with nice people.

Tina, Elena, and Adanna found themselves at the front porch of hell with no way out in sight. But they each would soon discover a light shining in the darkness.

Chapter 2

A RESCUE SHOP WITHIN
A YARD OF HELL

N O ORDINARY PERSON would ever plan to start a church in a red-light district, but Devaraj is not ordinary. Devaraj was working as an oil field executive in Iran in the waning days of the Shah's rule when he met an American pastor who invited him to a Bible study. Devaraj had recently arrived in Tehran from India. He was not very interested in the Bible study, but he wanted to make new friends, so he went. Devaraj found himself drawn to the people at the Bible study. They showed an outgoing love he had never seen. They cared about him as a person. Devaraj wasn't sure about Jesus being the unique Son of God, but these people were something special.

He kept going to the Bible study. Then he started attending the Sunday services. That special love kept him coming back. When student radicals over-turned the Shah, everyone in the church knew the American pastor would soon have to leave the country. Concerned about the fate of the little community of Jesus followers in such a hostile environment, Devaraj's pastor and mentor took him aside and told Devaraj that he needed to get baptized before the pastor departed. Devaraj had not had a dramatic conversion experience. He had never "accepted Jesus" as many American believers understood the concept. He had been overwhelmed by the love of Jesus' followers and had become part of their community. He did not hesitate. The pastor baptized Devaraj, then fled the country.

Devaraj stayed in Tehran for three years after the Americans left. One day he received a phone call from his American mentor, who invited Devaraj to join him in Beirut, where he was now serving. Devaraj accepted the invitation and spent the next four years in Lebanon, where he became involved with Teen Challenge, a global outreach founded by the Reverend David Wilkerson. Teen Challenge worked with troubled youth around the world. Many of those young people had been devastated by drugs or alcohol. Some had descended into a world of violence and demonism. Through the love of God and the power of the Holy Spirit, tens of thousands of those lost youth had experienced deliverance from every imaginable form of bondage and discovered lives of freedom, dignity, and purpose. If Devaraj learned about the love and power of Christian community in Tehran, he saw the power of the gospel demonstrated in Beirut.

The American pastor had watched Devaraj's growth

as a Jesus follower and believed the young man needed more formal ministry training. When conditions in Lebanon deteriorated in the late eighties, the pastor called me (David) and told me he had a student he wanted to send to Southern Asia Bible College (SABC) in Bangalore, India. He added, as a footnote, that the young man would need a scholarship. I didn't need to think it over. My response was immediate: "Tell him to come on!"

Devaraj did not want to return to India. The climate was too hot. The country was too poor. Devaraj wanted to go to Europe or America, where he could make money to support his family. And yet he had this persistent sense that God wanted him to return to India with all its problems.

Life at SABC was not pleasant. He found some of the professors pedantic. He was far too old to be a freshman in college. He wanted to quit and go back to the oil fields. But something kept him in school. While at SABC, Devaraj acquired a foundation of biblical and theological knowledge that would serve him well over the next thirty years.

When graduation day came, Devaraj took his young wife, Latijah, and moved to one of India's largest cities to start a Teen Challenge. He had seen the effectiveness of the ministry in Beirut to alcoholics and drug addicts. He felt God calling him to bring that same love to the streets of his new city. Early on, Devaraj began walking through the city's red-light district. The young preacher did not receive a warm welcome.

When the women working in the district discovered who he was, many of them averted their eyes, covered their faces, or shot him angry looks. His presence was not good for business.

The plight of the desperate young women trapped in the alleyways and hovels of the red-light district weighed heavily on Devaraj's heart. He and members of his team reached out to the young women and girls in the city's red-light district for years. From time to time, a young woman would come to Christ through their efforts. But the results were meager. Then a brothel owner came to Christ. Within a few weeks, most of the young women in her brothel also experienced the power of God to change a life. She started holding Saturday night services in the brothel. She soon offered to give the building to the ministry as a chapel.

Devaraj opened every service of the brothel church the same way: "Welcome to God's family," he would say, beaming, as he stretched his arms open to the women and their children.

Tina was one of those girls. In her early twenties by this time, she had seen this strange man walking the streets of the red-light district for years. He was not like any man she had ever seen. He did not look the girls up and down. He did not look at them like trash. It was his eyes and his smile that stood out. He always smiled. She wondered what his angle was. Every man had an angle. And yet those eyes were different.

She heard from some of the women in her brothel

that this man was holding some kind of meeting every Saturday evening. She decided to attend. It was an oppressively hot night when Tina attended for the first time. She had never really gotten used to the city's heat. She arrived just as the man stood to speak. His first words seemed strange to her: "Welcome to God's family." Tina did not know God had a family. Her family had sold her into this hell. Family? What good was family? Who needed family?

Then a group of girls began to sing, "I'm so glad Jesus set me free! I'm so glad Jesus set me free! I'm so glad Jesus set me free. Singing glory, hallelujah, Jesus set me free!" Some of them cried. Others raised their hands, their faces shining. Tina had never seen such a thing and certainly not in the red-light district. It was strange. She knew some of these girls. They had nothing to celebrate. She was sure some of them were dying from AIDS. How could they sing?

When they finished singing, a woman told everyone to share the love of Jesus before sitting down. One woman after the other came and hugged Tina and welcomed her to the family. Tina began to cry. She had not been hugged with love for more than ten years. It reminded her of her mother.

The smiling man, whom she later learned was called Uncle Devaraj, opened a black book. He read some words Tina had never heard, "For God so loved the world, that he gave his only begotten Son, that whosoever believeth in him should not perish, but have everlasting life" (John 3:16, KJV). The man explained

27

that God is not angry with us. He does not condemn us. He wants every one of us to enjoy His love, and He will change our lives if we ask Him to.

It seemed unbelievable. How could God change her life? Her gods had no ability to change a life. How could one God do this?

Tina left and went back to the brothel to work. She thought about the service all night. She had long ago learned to turn off her brain while she worked. This night was different. Even as she worked, she could feel that something was different. The songs the girls sang played on a continuous loop in her mind.

She went back the next Saturday night and the next. Tina attended every week. She soon began to take her son, Krishna, who was eight. He loved the singing. Tina cried when she saw her little boy clap his hands and sing the songs. He always bowed his head and prayed.

Little by little, Tina began to believe that this Jesus the man spoke about was real.

One Saturday night when Devaraj invited the participants to invite Jesus into their hearts, Tina decided she would accept the invitation. It was not hard to do. This safe place had become a real family to Tina and Krishna.

After the service, one of the women gave Tina a Bible. She clutched it to her heart even though she could not read it. She had heard Devaraj preach from the Bible for months. She loved its words. They brought her comfort and encouraged her.

Tina began to ask Jesus to take care of Krishna. She did not want her boy to grow up in the hell of the brothel. After praying about her son's future for some months, Tina started to feel that since Jesus had changed her life, she should give her son a Christian name. She talked with Krishna. He loved the story of a boy named Samuel who had heard the voice of God and served in God's house. She would talk to Uncle Devaraj. When Tina asked him what he thought, Devaraj smiled broadly and replied, "I think this is a perfect name," as he patted Krishna's head.

Then Tina felt a prayer bubbling out of her. "Pastor, can you take Samuel away from this hell? Can you give him a new place to live, away from this?" She wiped her eyes with her sari as she spoke. In the days to come, a number of the ladies of the church would make similar requests of Devaraj.

What she could not know was that Devaraj had made a telephone call that would change Samuel's life and the lives of scores of other children in the red-light district. Devaraj had called me (David) and told me about what God was doing in the red-light district.

I had known the city for more than thirty years. I had been shocked by it as a young man and wept over it more times than I could remember. But in 1997, after receiving the call from Devaraj, I made my own visit to the front porch of hell.

It was unbelievable.

Devaraj took me to the red-light district late one night. The streets were jammed with men of all ages.

New Orleans during Mardi Gras is not more crowded than the streets were that night. Young women lounged in the doorways as a river of men flowed past them. I was struck by the eyes of these women and girls. Their eyes were dead. No matter how old they were or how they were dressed, their eyes were all the same. I fought back tears.

What I saw that night has haunted me for a quarter of a century. Young girls—some as young as seven or eight years old—were being trafficked to men. I felt like someone had hit me in the stomach. It took my breath away. Devaraj told me that more than one hundred thousand children in the city lived in this hell, forced by pimps to service as many as twenty men every night. Many of them would die of AIDS before they were twenty-one. Those who survived would be scarred forever by the physical and sexual abuse they experienced every day. This was a level of deprivation and abuse I could not conceive of.

And yet in the midst of the darkness, God was showing Himself great on behalf of these broken, bruised, and marginalized women and their children. I remember when a madam called Devaraj and said, "You're taking little babies, little girls, to your Home of Hope. Here's a three-year-old you can have. Her nineteen-year-old mother died of AIDS yesterday. The child was born with AIDS. She's going to die. You can have her."

Six months later our staff doctor called and said, "I tested the three-year-old this morning, and there's not a trace of the virus left in her body. Jesus has healed her of AIDS."

She was not the only child or woman to experience God's miraculous power to heal and restore.

I was in the brothel church a few months later, and a nineteen-year-old girl stood to testify. "My father sold me for two hundred dollars when I was twelve years old," she said slowly and softly. "I have been raped, beaten, and brutalized for seven years, but Jesus brought me out."

She went on to testify, "He has healed the scars in my mind and healed the memories of seven years of hell. He has taken out the heart of stone." Then she made a statement that caused the room to go silent: "He has washed my blood of the virus that was killing me. My blood is clean; my mind is free."

There is no understanding Project Rescue, the ministry that began through Devaraj's outreach to the women being prostituted in the red-light district, apart from the supernatural power of God to rescue, heal, and restore. Project Rescue is a supernatural ministry. Every Project Rescue leader has stories of miraculous healings, restoration, and divine appointments—like the one Elena had in a Paris café.

RUNNING TOWARD FREEDOM

The days and weeks after Elena arrived in Antwerp were an unending horror show of torture and abuse. Elena was a good girl. Her mother and grandmother were serious Orthodox believers who went to the church regularly to pray. They celebrated all the holy days on the calendar. Elena's favorite was Pascha, or Easter as it is called in the West. She and her mom painted eggs, baked the Pascha bread, bought a special Ukrainian wine, and went to the church, where the priest blessed it and sprinkled them with water. It was one of the best days of the year, second only to the New Year. Her mother and grandmother instilled strong values in her. Elena was an excellent student who usually stood at or near the head of her class. She practiced her piano. She dreamed the dreams girls all over the world dreamed.

Ukrainians had suffered too much during communism and the Second World War to expect life to be easy. Life was certainly not easy in Ukraine, but most Ukrainians believed that eventually life would be better. What Elena was experiencing was something else altogether.

When the man told her she had to "earn her keep," Elena knew what he meant. And she determined that she wasn't going to be a prostitute. Her grandmother told her that prostitutes were lazy girls with no character. They wouldn't pay attention to their studies. They smoked, drank, and used drugs. That was not who Mama raised her to be. When the man came back a few hours later and told her to get ready for work, Elena refused. He slapped her across the face. It knocked her to the floor. Then he kicked her. He called her terrible names. Elena curled up into a fetal position. He took the cigarette out of his mouth and burned her arm. Later he drugged her. He made it clear enough that he would be happy to kill her and have people in Ukraine kill her mother and grandmother. Elena had no doubt that a Mafia guy like Oleg would kill her like a dog. Finally, she gave in.

A couple of days later, Oleg told her to get dressed. Tatiana gave her a short black skirt, a red blouse, black stockings, and black stilettos. She took the clothes to the bathroom and dressed. Tatiana did her makeup. Elena did not recognize the girl in the mirror. She looked like something she had seen in the movies, something she did not want to be. Elena was sick to her stomach.

Oleg drove her to a hotel near the city center. The city was gray and foreboding. The light drizzle made it worse.

When they arrived at the hotel, Oleg took Elena through the gold revolving door and through the lobby to the elevators. Oleg gave her the room number and told her to come back in an hour.

"Time is money. Don't give anything away."

Elena nervously entered the elevator and hesitantly pressed the button for the eighth floor. She felt the swoosh of the elevator as it glided upward. A moment later it stopped suddenly, the doors opened, and Elena walked down the hall. She knocked on the door. A man of about fifty-five years came to the door. He was obviously drunk. Elena had seen enough drunks on the street and in restaurants. She shivered at the thought of being alone with such a person.

He told her to lie on the bed as he began taking off his clothes. Elena closed her eyes tightly and prepared herself. She wasn't responsive, and the man was not happy. He cursed her through gritted teeth and slapped her. He called her a cheat and other terrible names. By the time she dressed herself and got back to the lobby, Oleg had already received a call from Tatiana. His eyes were burning coals of hatred and contempt.

When they returned to the apartment, he practically threw her in the door. This time he punched her in the mouth—twice. She fell to the floor, just as she had her first day in the apartment. He kicked her again and again. The pain went through her like a fire. Then Elena lost consciousness.

Elena learned in her first forty-eight hours in Antwerp that resistance was pointless. It would get her hurt or worse. Now the point was to survive. Like trafficked women around the world, Elena learned to get by.

The next five years were a treadmill of appointments. Sometimes the clients treated her kindly. A few were mean or depraved. Most made no particular impression on her, forgotten almost as soon as she left their hotel rooms. Most of the time Elena blocked it all out to let her mind wander to better places; then it didn't hurt so bad. She also started drinking. At first it was a glass of wine with a client, but over time Elena drank more, sometimes until she passed out. She took pills every day. Something in her began to die. Her kindness, her sense of humor, her appreciation of beauty all became faded, like an old, worn-out pair of jeans. In fact, more and more, Elena felt faded, hollowed out. She was slowly ceasing to be human.

One afternoon Elena was sitting in a hotel café when she met a nice woman from Poland, who asked her how she was doing. No one ever asked Elena how she was doing. No one in the apartment cared, not Tatiana and certainly not Oleg. But this woman had kind eyes, like her mama's. Somehow it seemed that she cared.

Still, Elena looked at her warily. Was she police or from some social agency? She didn't look like the police. Elena looked at her vacantly and replied, "So-so." Then it was time for Elena to go.

She saw the woman a few weeks later, and again she asked Elena, "How are you today?"

For some reason, the words tumbled out: "Sometimes I want to die."

The woman quietly took a card out of her purse and moved it across the table. "This is my card. Call me if you would like to talk." The woman's name was Maria, like Mary the mother of God. Elena could feel a mother's love from her.

Still on guard, she thanked the woman and said she would call sometime. For the first time in years, Elena felt love. It was a few days before she found a way to safely make the call. Maria answered on the first ring.

"Maria, this is Elena. Can you get me out?"

The question needed no elaboration.

"Yes, of course," Maria said quietly but firmly.

"I know how to come down a service elevator where no one will see me. Can you be there at six o'clock tonight?" Elena shook with fear. She knew what Oleg did to girls who tried to escape. If he caught her, she would be lucky if all he did was beat her. She knew that Oleg would kill her without remorse or pity. She went to the kitchen of the apartment and threw back a few ounces of whiskey. It burned, but it settled her nerves.

That afternoon Elena went to the hotel, as she often did. She was going to see one of her regulars, a nice man from Germany who came to Antwerp every few weeks. She would feign a headache; he would willingly let her leave a few minutes early.

Everything ran according to plan. She went to the service elevator on the tenth floor and took a deep breath. She pushed the button. She waited for what seemed like a lifetime. She knew Oleg would be in the bar drinking vodka. Finally, the old elevator made its way to the tenth floor. Elena looked furtively left and then right. Then she took a quick step to freedom.

When she stepped out of a side entrance to the hotel, she saw a van and Maria standing on the curb with an open umbrella. Raindrops trickled from the sides of the umbrella. Elena picked up her pace, her stilettos rhythmically striking the sidewalk. Maria slid the door open. Elena stepped into the van and slumped into the seat. Maria put her arm around her shoulders and said, "Welcome, my dear; you are safe now."

Touched by the Father's Love

Don Valdez visited Adanna whenever the Doña and the children were away. Adanna survived by going to her Nigerian church. She felt the presence of God whenever she went to the church. Adanna had no way of knowing the pastor's wife trafficked girls. She told Adanna and some other Nigerian girls that God would forgive them every week for the sins they committed with their bodies and protect them from curses, getting caught by the police, or contracting AIDS. Something felt wrong to Adanna. Over the next several months, she visited other churches.

One Sunday, Adanna attended a church where the pastor told the congregation they had a special guest, Fiona Bellshaw. The pastor said God had sent her to Spain to rescue young women trapped in prostitution and sexual exploitation. Adanna leaned forward as Fiona spoke. She talked about how procurers tricked young girls in Africa to come to Spain as domestic workers or nannies but then forced them to become sex workers. Fiona talked about God's love for the victims and told the congregation how God helped the victims live beyond shame. She spoke about the homes God had helped them open in Madrid and other cities in Spain. She talked about how the government supported their efforts financially and legally.

It seemed that Fiona's every word was aimed at Adanna's heart. When Fiona finished speaking, the pastor invited the congregation forward for prayer. Adanna rose from her chair and walked to the front. Fiona came to her and put her arms around her. Adanna had not felt such love since her mother hugged her on the day she left Benin City. Fiona offered a simple prayer, "Father, You know the pain in this girl's heart. Please cause her to feel Your love." One tear fell on Adanna's cheek, then another. It was as if God had put His finger on her heart and was draining the pain. Adanna stood at the front for a while. When she opened her eyes, she felt different—clean, free. She also knew what she needed to do. Fiona was talking with the pastor. Adanna waited patiently until Fiona came to her.

"How can I help you, my dear?" Fiona asked.

Adanna explained her situation. "I need to get away." She felt bad. She cared for the Doña and the children. The Doña had always been kind. But Don Valdez frightened her. She had to escape.

Fiona asked her if she was ready to go. Adanna nodded her head. She went to the center with Fiona that afternoon. She never saw the Valdez family again.

Real estate investors often say the key to real estate is "Location, location, location." It is true in ministry as well. British missionary C. T. Studd once wrote, "Some wish to live within the sound of church or chapel bell; I want to run a rescue shop within a yard of hell."[1] Where is the best place for a ministry to those in great darkness? It is as Studd said—within a yard of hell. Project Rescue has reaped a harvest among the victims of sex trafficking unheard of in two thousand years of Christian missions. Visitors to Project Rescue ministry centers always want to know the secret. It's location.

Chapter 3

THE WAY OUT

THE AASHAGRAM AFTERCARE ministry is a far cry from the horrors of the red-light district. It is a place where the eyes of young girls dance with delight, a place where hearts and minds are healed. Aashagram, the "Village of Hope," has become the way out for hundreds of women and their children, a place where they have found life beyond the red-light district. It is a community of safety, healing, and restoration.

Project Rescue has established Homes of Hope in South Asia and Europe, safe houses where the victims have time and space to heal.

The road to health and wholeness for women like Tina, Elena, and Adanna is usually long because of the horror they have suffered and the trauma to their bodies, minds, and hearts. Brain scientists tell us that oftentimes social and emotional development stop at the point of the trauma. So even though a young woman may be twenty-three when she enters a Project

Rescue home, she may be eight or nine years old emotionally. Also, she has been manipulated so long that she has learned to manipulate others. Manipulation becomes a way of life. The process of healing and growing socially and emotionally never takes less than a year. Some women have been so traumatized by torture and abuse it may take them a year to be able to speak to a man.

This came home to Rod Loy, an Assemblies of God pastor in Arkansas, when he visited Moldova in 2011. "I sat in the Project Rescue homes and laughed and talked with the girls," he said. "My biggest takeaway was the incredible amount of time it takes to help a person find healing. It is a grueling, time-consuming, emotionally draining process. It's just what it takes. Many of them were sold at age ten or eleven. We cannot imagine the depth of the trauma."[1]

RESCUE

The path for every young woman or girl is as unique as they are, but through twenty-five years of working with thousands of young women, a process took shape. It starts with rescue, extracting the victim from continued abuse and the trauma it causes. The victims of sex trafficking need to make a complete break from that life whenever possible and move into an environment that is physically and psychologically safe. They have been exploited and brutalized for years; their first need is to move into an environment where God can restore them.

Young women like Elena and Adanna know this intuitively. They understand that their environment pulls them down and keeps them down. Escape is not an option; it is necessary to their survival. In most cases they have dreamed of getting out of the life for years. They hate it and everything about it, including themselves. Project Rescue team members become God's means of escape.

But each woman herself is an active participant in the process. Take Jumana, for instance. She was considered the lowest of the low, "garbage" among those in sexual slavery. Even red-light districts have their own hierarchy, and her dark skin made her less desirable to the men who visited the brothel where she lived. She had nowhere to go, no way of escape, because she had been trafficked from another country. One day Jumana quietly entered the door of the Project Rescue vocational center at the edge of the district with her head bowed, unable to look up because of her shame. She was warmly welcomed by staff. Though shattered by abuse, Jumana was still an active agent in coming out of bondage.

RESTORATION

When we talk about restoration, we are talking about restoring human dignity, part of what the Hebrew Scriptures call the image of God, which has been shattered by exploitation and abuse. That restoration can happen only in an atmosphere of love, acceptance, and forgiveness—in short, in a family. Family is God's gift to humans, the place where we learn that we are loved, cared for, and safe; it's the place where we learn how to build relationships. Many of the women and girls who come to Project Rescue have had their understanding of family shredded by the experience of trafficking if they ever had lived in a healthy family. A girl of eight or nine may not have understood what was happening to her when she was sold into a brothel, but eventually she did. That realization destroyed all trust. Young women like Elena have been betrayed by "lover boys" who played on their emotions and then exploited them. As a result, they come to believe men cannot be trusted.

Fiona Bellshaw maintains that the Slavic girls who come to the home in Madrid are the most vulnerable of all because so many of them grew up without fathers. "The girls who come from Eastern Europe are completely unprotected. In South America, the strong families provide protection. The Slavic girls have no one." That is why we have "homes" and outreaches that feel like "family," where girls can come "home."

Project Rescue is saturated in love. Whether it is Devaraj welcoming women to God's family in the Saturday night service or a meeting in an Antwerp café, love is at the heart of Project Rescue's ministry—an outgoing, overflowing love that breaks through the walls of betrayal, distrust, and fear. Whatever else the thousands of women and girls who have been touched by Project Rescue may say, they all talk about the love. It is as different from the world they have known as darkness and light. It is the embodiment of the words of the apostle John, "Perfect love drives out fear" (1 John 4:18).

The young women and girls enter an atmosphere suffused with the Word of God so they can experience what the apostle Paul called "the washing of water by the word," where they can "be transformed by the renewing of [their] mind" (Eph. 5:26, KJV; Rom. 12:2). It is difficult to help someone who has not been there to understand the levels of trauma and the depths of humiliation victims of sexual exploitation experience. The women are taught to begin every day by entering God's presence with praise and worship and to "pray without ceasing" (1 Thess. 5:17, KJV) as they face the challenges of putting their lives together. It's what the apostle Paul called "put[ting] on the Lord Jesus Christ" (Rom. 13:14, NKJV).

Restoration is, first and foremost, a spiritual journey. It starts when a young woman decides to follow Jesus and live for Him. Many women living in Homes of Hope discover other dimensions of help and healing and have not yet made the decision to follow Jesus. Becoming a Jesus follower is always a choice. But when a woman makes that choice, she becomes a "new creation" (2 Cor. 5:17). Restoration is not reconstruction or self-improvement; it is self-replacement, as the apostle Paul explained to a group of new Jesus followers who lived in a depraved, pagan environment. "It is no longer I who live, but Christ who lives in me," Paul wrote. "And the life I now live in the flesh I live by faith in the Son of God, who loved me and gave himself for me" (Gal. 2:20, ESV).

That journey is a combination of event and process.

When Jumana came to the vocational center, she could not believe the women there welcomed and accepted her. Her sense of shame and rejection was so great that she did not believe she was worthy to sit and learn with them. So Jumana offered to clean toilets if they would just allow her to join them. Team members firmly declined and assured her they wanted her to join them for devotions and training sessions, where she would learn to stitch or whatever skill she most desired to pick up.

One day as one team member was praying for Jumana and seeking God's wisdom to help her, God spoke to the person and said, "Ask Jumana about her name." The next time this team member encountered Jumana at the center, she said, "Jumana, tell me about your name!"

Jumana said, "It's the name of a great river in my home country that is so pure and clean. People try to live as close to the river as possible, because wherever the river flows, there is life and growth!" In that God moment, our colleague spoke over Jumana, "Because of Jesus, you will become like that beautiful river—pure, clean, full of life. You will be life and joy to all you meet! You will be Jumana!"

The eyes of this devastated woman who had been so filled with hurt and shame began to shine. She smiled, and her face lit up as she embraced the words of hope and faith spoken over her. She said her name out loud, over and over again, until she was laughing with joy.

The chains of spiritual darkness over Jumana snapped that day, and she became a source of joy and peace to those in the red-light district and to her new friends in the nearby vocational center, where she now worked serving others in every way she possibly could. Women like Jumana carry distorted images of themselves and the world that need to be transformed so they can see themselves through the lens of God's truth and love. It is sadly common for a girl to hear these words from her mother: "Your grandmother was a prostitute. I am a prostitute. You will be what I am." In some villages in South Asia, girls have been raised for prostitution for hundreds of years. They live on the margins of the village without status or property. They are despised. During two hundred years of British colonialism, the British Army routinely recruited girls from these villages for the comfort of officers and enlisted men. These destructive mindsets have to be replaced so these young women can experience transformation.

Recently Devaraj sat down in a New York café with a prominent businessman. The man asked Devaraj about Project Rescue's success rate. Without blinking, Devaraj told him that 90 percent of the young women who come through Project Rescue do not go back to the streets. The man looked at Devaraj and said, "Ninety percent? I would have thought 30 or 40 percent." Neither Devaraj nor any other Project Rescue leader is the key to that success; spiritual transformation is the key.

But while the spiritual transformation resulting from a spiritual new birth is foundational and essential, the spiritual alone is not enough. Most of the village girls come to Homes of Hope with little or no education. Few of them can read. Learning to read is one of the most important steps to becoming Spirit-empowered women. This is why every Home of Hope prioritizes teaching preliterate women and girls to read.

Vocational training is critical for a new life. The young women who come to Project Rescue have no marketable skills, whether they come from South Asia, Eastern Europe, or Africa. Part of the restoration process is to help every girl identify her God-given talents and develop the knowledge, skills, and attitudes that will enable her to become successful. As early as 1998, Devaraj dreamed of a center where the young women could be educated and receive technical training. The dream became Aashagram, the Village of Hope. After a young woman leaves the red-light district, she goes to Aashagram, where she learns a trade so she can earn a steady income. Education and vocational training ensure that the young women who come out of prostitution stay out and their children stay out. It is nothing less than creating a new future and destiny for a woman and her children.

Some women within the church and local communities feel called to work in the Village of Hope. But many of the workers in Mumbai have come out of the red-light district. The madam who sold her brothel to Project Rescue is now a minister. So is her daughter. Some of the women transformed through Project Rescue have been sent to Southern Asia Bible College to gain competency in understanding the Scriptures and applying them to life. Most of the young women in Project Rescue homes in South Asia never dreamed of going to college or university. At Aashagram hundreds of young women have learned to design jewelry or handbags. Some have become seamstresses. Each one of them has been given the opportunity to gain the sense of dignity, self-worth, and self-sufficiency that come from meaningful work.

Restoration is hard, grueling work. It cannot be done by remote control. It is hands-on and inherently relational. Exploited women and girls have been shattered by life. Their psyches are in pieces. It takes loving patience and time for them to become whole again.

REENTRY

The process of restoration is complete when a young woman enters society as a fully Spirit-empowered woman who can support herself and becomes an agent of healing for others. The apostle Paul spoke to a group of Corinthian believers notorious for their self-centeredness and reminded them that "He died for all, that those who live should no longer live for themselves but for him who died for them and was raised again....All this is from God, who reconciled us to himself through Christ and gave us the ministry of reconciliation" (2 Cor. 5:15, 18).

The women and girls whose lives have been changed through the ministry of Project Rescue are evidence that the gospel works, transformation is possible, and a girl can live beyond the humiliation, shame, and disgrace of prostitution and sexual exploitation.

PREVENTION

A wise man once said, "It's better to build a fence at the top of a hill than park an ambulance at the bottom." Prevention has been a critical element in Project Rescue's strategy from its inception.

Beginning in 1998, teams went into towns and villages of Nepal and India and distributed *Edward the Elephant*, a comic book addressing HIV/AIDS and helping children develop the knowledge, skills, and attitudes to protect themselves from traffickers.

The initial impulse for prevention came from the

young women who begged Devaraj to take their children twenty-five years ago. "It's too late for us; please take our children," they pleaded. The Project Rescue children's homes came in response to the cries from mothers who didn't want their children to live in the hell they had known.

Project Rescue homes have been lifelines for children whose mothers work in red-light districts—children like Kani.

As the cries of a newborn baby filled a hospital room, the mother who had just given birth to this baby girl walked out of the hospital and didn't look back. Sadly, within the first few minutes of her life, Kani was abandoned by her mother. Though her grandmother was very poor, she agreed to take Kani in, raising her in the red-light district.

Four years later Kani's mother, who was prostituted in the red-light district, demanded that Kani be returned to her. Without any love in her heart for her daughter, the mother treated Kani like a servant, forcing her to clean the house, wash the clothes, shop for food, and fetch water at 5:00 a.m.

At five years old, Kani lost her innocence when her uncles and other outsiders began sexually abusing her, forcing her to sit on their laps while they touched her inappropriately. If she voiced this to her mother, her mother would scold and beat her. A year or so later, her aunt began taking Kani with her to see customers with the intent to "groom" her, all while making plans to adopt Kani so she could then sell her.

The abuse continued and intensified. At one point when Kani was alone with her uncle, he suddenly grabbed her, threw her on the bed, stuffed a handkerchief in her mouth, and tried to rape her. Fighting against the weight of her uncle, she bit him, which enraged him even more. He grabbed a large stone grinder and hurled it at her, barely missing her as she fled from the home completely naked.

Horrific situations continued to happen in Kani's life until she was seven years old. At that time she started attending a Project Rescue after-school program, where she was surrounded by people who loved her and wanted her to flourish. For the first time since she was born, Kani felt loved.

Soon after, Project Rescue launched a shelter for girls, and after much convincing, Kani's mother allowed her to go. Kani's mother watched as she grew and thrived, and her heart began to soften. In the subsequent years Kani's aunt told her mother emphatically, "Take her back and sell her. You'll make a lot more money."

Seeing that her daughter had a future at the Project Rescue home, Kani's mother refused to take her back and instead wrote a letter to Project Rescue, ensuring that her daughter would never be taken from the home.

A few years later during a church service, Kani encountered the Lord in a supernatural way, and He began healing the wounds and trauma that haunted her life. Leaving transformed, Kani developed a better relationship with her mother, and it grew over time. A month before her mother passed away, Kani spent the holidays with her, feeling love and care from her mother that she had never experienced before.

Kani now works at the Project Rescue boys' and girls' homes as part of the residential staff. Her heart's passion is to walk alongside children growing up in similar situations as she did. Her story may not have had a good beginning, but the end of her story has already been written—a beautiful inscription in the Book of Life.

Measuring the Results

We live in a society where people want to see the metrics, where every program is measured to determine its effectiveness. The ultimate measure of Project Rescue's strategy lies in the lives of the thousands of women and children who have received life-changing ministry over the last twenty-five years. On average, Project Rescue impacts as many as fifty thousand women and children each year.

Few outreaches to the victims of sex trafficking have been more effective in rescue and restoration than Project Rescue. That success is rooted in a process that works in every nation and culture. It works not because the Project Rescue team is more talented, innovative, or dedicated than those who serve in similar ministries. It works because the gospel works. It works because when the gospel is applied to human suffering with love and patience, the result is more powerful than any problem people have. It is, as the apostle Paul declared to new believers in ancient Rome, "the power of God that brings salvation to everyone who believes" (Rom. 1:16).

Chapter 4

THE DARK WORLD OF SEX TRAFFICKING

M ORE THAN ONE million girls have been sold or kidnapped into prostitution in the nations of South Asia, a number almost impossible to comprehend. But while Project Rescue started in that region, sex trafficking is a global scandal, a vast multinational business destroying the lives of no less than four million young women, men, and children. The world of trafficking is not black, white, or brown. It is not the particular scourge of underdeveloped countries. It is everywhere, including the place where you live.

Pimps from all over the world buy and sell young girls and women. Experts estimate that ten million girls in two hundred nations have been sold into prostitution. Girls from Russia and Ukraine fill the brothels of Western Europe and the United States. Traffickers import tens of thousands of young women from Africa and South America into Europe every year on false passports. Prostitution enslaves more women and children than any other form of slavery in human history. Millions of women and girls live in bondage, terror, and torture.

Global estimates of the number of sex trafficking victims are known to be conservative and are difficult to substantiate. Victims underreport out of fear of the traffickers. They are held in bondage by intimidation, violence, and threats of death against them and their families. Most of them do not trust law enforcement or the justice system. And then there is the shame attached to prostitution.

Sex trafficking may be out of sight in a city or town or in plain sight in strip malls, in storefronts, next door to the Asian grocery store, or in the nail salon advertising "Massage." And except for the occasional bust by local law enforcement, the traffickers operate with impunity. The exorbitant profits to criminal syndicates more than justify the risks. The occasional arrest is nothing more than a cost of doing business.

Sex trafficking involves vast, highly organized, complex webs of criminal conspiracy. Every country has its mafias that prey on the naïve and unsuspecting. But the industry also includes the freelancer who traffics his own children or runaways.

REAL GIRLS, REAL DAUGHTERS

More than forty years ago a Spirit-empowered vice cop in Minneapolis broke the "Minnesota Connection," a pipeline of teenage runaways recruited or kidnapped in the Twin Cities and shipped to New York to supply pimps and customers with "those Scandinavian girls." The story became a best-selling book and a made-for-TV movie. Already a compelling story, it was made all the more attractive because the girls were blue-eyed blondes from the American heartland.

The vice cop went on to found a ministry of safe houses in several cities that did a great work. But it was not the full picture. The victims of sex trafficking have often been runaways. Many of them have been victimized or sold by parents or family members. They run because there is enough space in America for them to simply get lost in the crowd.

The vast majority of trafficked women have stories like Tina's, Elena's, and Adanna's. They are the victims of war, poverty, and social class. They have no standing and no protection. In many cases they have no family. If they disappear, it does not matter because they do not exist to anyone outside their own homes, if they are even noticed there.

Age is not a protection. Women of middle age are recruited in China, Korea, and Thailand to work in massage parlors in the United States, where no one can help them. These women are completely isolated and moved every couple of months to a new location to keep them off the grid.

The victims do not all come from grinding poverty either. Pastor Rod Loy sat in a McDonald's in Moldova with a pastor's daughter who had been trafficked. Loy better understood the plight of the victims in that moment. "These are real girls," he said. "These are real daughters. They never chose this. They never wanted this."[1] This is the heart of the matter. The victims are not statistics; they are real girls, real women.

THE FACES OF SEX TRAFFICKING

The stories of Tina, Elena, and Adanna put human faces on the statistics. Every trafficked woman or girl is some mother's daughter, a person created in God's likeness and image. They carry the fingerprints of the eternal God on their hearts and minds. In his vision of God's eternal throne, Ezekiel saw cherubim who had "the face of a human being" (Ezek. 1:10), which suggests that the faces we see in our world are patterned after beings who live in the presence of God. Nothing speaks more clearly to the sacredness of human life or to the abomination of trafficking than the faces around the throne.

Some advocates of legalizing prostitution in the liberal democracies of the West describe it as a "victimless crime." This is a superficial view that lacks moral seriousness and ignores the human toll of sex trafficking on everyone involved—on its young victims, whose innocence and dignity are ground into the dirt every day; on the procurers and pimps, who lose any sense of caring or compassion; and on the customers, for whom sex becomes a consumer item instead of the doorway to intimacy God designed it to be. Project

Rescue gives voices to women and girls who would otherwise be used and discarded by the traffickers like any other disposable commodity.

UNDERSTANDING THE VICTIMS

Understanding and ministering to the victims of sex trafficking is often inhibited by the cultures in which the victims find themselves. In Spain, attitudes toward sex and sexuality translate into either acceptance or tolerance of behavior like Don Valdez's toward Adanna. Some villages in South Asia have been seedbeds of prostitution for hundreds of years. Women and girls in some villages have been raised to be prostitutes, as were their mothers and grandmothers before them. They do not question their situation. It is their fate.

In many developing countries, the girl child is seen as a curse or a burden. A boy holds the promise of building the family, of increasing its wealth and standing in the community. A baby girl is a burden, another mouth to feed. If the family loses income due to a hurricane, earthquake, or tsunami, the parents often conclude that they cannot care for the girl. She will be sold so there is one less child to support. Most of the girls who land in the red-light districts of South Asia are sold for economic reasons.

Culture, religion, and superstitions complicate the situation and sometimes foster sexual exploitation. It's not uncommon for cultures throughout the world to put a premium on having sex with a virgin, the younger the better. Men pay top dollar to have access to girls as young as seven years old. There is a goddess of prostitution in South Asia to whom girl children are often dedicated. Prostitution in the name of religion can be found around the world.

Christian churches are not exempt from attitudes contrary to the gospel. Many pastors believe prostitution is a choice. They believe that once a young woman "repents," all she has to do is "choose" to leave the life. If only it were that easy. The vast majority of women trapped in prostitution want to get out, but they owe debts they can never repay. Like Adanna, some "owe" as much as $55,000. They are owned by their pimps. Many of these young women have been so shattered by trauma and abuse that they cannot make good choices. They need rescue and total restoration.

Many church leaders around the world see discipleship as a three-step process in which people are taught first to *believe*, then to *behave*, and then finally to *belong*. It is a perfectly logical model and one prevalent in every religious tradition. It is just not the Jesus model. He turned this equation on its head. He invited people to join Him. He spent time with them and shared His life with them. They went where He went, ate what He ate, and slept where He slept. They watched what He did, heard His words, and came to believe in Him. Over time they learned to live differently. It was a long process that took three and a half years with the first cohort. But it worked. Instead of a religion, Jesus founded a movement that changed the world. And the Jesus model has been the approach in every Project Rescue outreach.

April Foster, Shawn Alderman, and their team routinely visit Antwerp's red-light district and give tea or coffee to the young women working in its 274 windows. They make friends. They invite the women to visit the Oasis Center. Acceptance and friendship open the door to the gospel.

Project Rescue has worked with pastors and church leaders around the globe to help them understand the heart of the Father for the oppressed and come to a more biblical understanding of how the church ministers grace and freedom to the victims of sexual slavery. Today, churches around the world offer trafficked women and their children the love and acceptance they need to experience full rescue and restoration.

Project Rescue has also worked with pastors and church leaders in America, Europe, and Africa to help them understand the real issues at work in sex trafficking. One African bishop wept openly when he saw young women from his country being forced to sell themselves for sex on the streets in Madrid. "These are my people!" he exclaimed. Perhaps the work of bringing understanding to church leaders around the world represents one of the least publicized but most important achievements of the ministry.

SUPPLY AND DEMAND

Finally, there would be no sex trafficking or exploitation without the men who live in their own bondage. They are driven by impulses and desires that destroy God's image in them as surely and certainly as they destroy it in the victims.

When people awaken to the issues of sex trafficking and exploitation, the initial response is often anger. Some people want to physically confront those who contribute to the more than $200 billion global sex industry. As Jesus followers we always need to remember that both the patron and the trafficker need God to change their lives.

Years ago on an overseas visit, an American pastor joined Project Rescue for the red-light district outreach. His response was not typical for an American seeing the horror for the first time. He had pity on the men of the district and said, "Every man knocking on the door of a brothel is searching for something or perhaps trying to fill a void in their lives that can only be satisfied by the God who created them." Project Rescue team members share this belief and minister accordingly. This can be difficult to accept, but God's love is not reserved for the victims only. His love extends to all, even to traffickers.

Believers around the world sing the words of "Amazing Grace":

> Amazing grace! how sweet the sound,
> That saved a wretch; like me!

I once was lost, but now am found,
Was blind, but now I see.[2]

The words of this beloved and most widely quoted hymn were written by a human trafficker, John Newton, who bought and sold slaves from Africa.

Forever Free

During the COVID-19 crisis, Project Rescue launched the Forever Free project, which provides vocational training to women to give them a pathway out of the red-light district.

Project Rescue team leaders saw a unique opportunity to impact the male traffickers who work in the red-light community too. The local Project Rescue director met with the general contractor and informed him that the workers for this construction project would need to be men from the local villages. Many of the construction workers were known traffickers or patrons.

The ministry leader recognized that men in these villages needed not only work but also a chance to connect with the God who loves them. One of the young men shared that he never wanted to be involved with trafficking, but due to his family history he felt compelled to do so.

One of our leaders gave a Bible to a trafficker. Weeks later the man testified that he had searched the gods of other religions all his life and felt nothing. He went on to say, "When I read the Bible, something in my heart leaped!" God can move the heart of the trafficker. God can move in the hearts of those who exploit. It is our job to give God a chance to do what only He can do.

Chapter 5

THE HEART OF THE MINISTRY

I (DAVID) OFTEN PREACH a sermon with three simple points: "I know who I am, I know where I'm going, and I'm not going by myself." These are not just pithy sayings; these are core values for us. Beth often says that when you become involved in the ministry of rescuing and restoring the victims of sexual slavery, you are storming the very gates of hell. If you do not know who you are and why you are doing what you do, you are bound to fail.

Discussions about core values should never be arcane and academic; understanding and walking out certain core values is at the heart of all ministry, especially ministry to women and girls whose lives have been devastated by trafficking. The person who does not minister out of certain core values will be at the mercy of the urgent or paralyzed by their failures. They will do some good, but they will not accomplish what they could if they had been more thoughtful and strategic. All ministries operate from their core values.

In the early days of Project Rescue, our core values were more implicit than explicit, in part because most of the team came from the same ethos of Spirit-empowered Christianity. We grew up singing the same hymns and learning the same Sunday school lessons. Many of us went to the same colleges. Today that is no longer true. The Project Rescue team comes from many cultures and many different backgrounds. To be effective in ministry together, we must know what we believe and what we are committed to.

After twenty-five years of ministry to broken young women and children—twenty-five years of victories and defeats, of stunning breakthroughs and heart-breaking disappointments—the Project Rescue team has identified five core values that define who we are and why we do what we do. These values provide the GPS for ministering to victims of sexual slavery, and they set the overall direction of the ministry. We have sought to ground these values in (1) the Scriptures, which alone "make [us] wise unto salvation" (2 Tim. 3:15, KJV); (2) twenty centuries of Christian life and Spirit-empowered witness; and (3) the real-life experience of millions of Jesus followers in "every nation and in every tongue." (See Revelation 7:9.)

1. We Are Jesus-Centered

Perhaps it should go without saying, but Jesus is the center of everything Project Rescue does. He is "the way, the truth, and the life" (John 14:6, KJV), who alone can set the captives free—physically, mentally, emotionally, spiritually—and bring people into fellowship with the Father. He is more than a concept or a set of theological truths; He is a living person. As He Himself said to the apostle John in the opening words of Revelation, "I am the Alpha and the Omega...who is, and who was, and who is to come, the Almighty" (Rev. 1:8). He is the One who, at the end of history, will be "all in all" (1 Cor. 15:28).

The Jesus we proclaim is a historical figure, but He is also a living reality who still says and does everything He ever said and did. That is why the writer of Hebrews could say, "Jesus Christ is the same yesterday and today and forever" (Heb. 13:8).

The ministry of Project Rescue is all about Jesus. It is about who He is, what He has done, and what He is doing in the world today. One team member reflected on ministry in secular Europe, where few people know much about Jesus. Many of the young women in their outreach center come from parts of the world where most people do not view Jesus as the unique Son of God. "We live Jesus," she said. "We do what Jesus does, say what Jesus says, and pray the way Jesus prayed."

Losing focus is one of the occupational hazards of ministry, to get so caught up in the daily grind that Jesus becomes secondary and the work becomes primary. Project Rescue team members know that without Jesus they have nothing to give and no hope to offer. But because they are connected to Him, the words of Jesus have become a renewable energy source in some of the darkest, most difficult places on earth, just as Jesus promised:

> But whoever drinks the water I give them will never thirst. Indeed, the water I give them will become in them a spring of water welling up to eternal life.
>
> —JOHN 4:14

> He that believeth on me, as the scripture hath said, out of his belly shall flow rivers of living water.
>
> —JOHN 7:38, KJV

Once you get clear about who Jesus is and what He has done, the rest is details. You learn to live in the "power of his resurrection, and the fellowship of his sufferings" (Phil. 3:10, KJV), no matter what happens around you. If Jesus is not the center, the oppressive darkness of the world of sex trafficking has a way of closing in on you. Sociology, politics, and corruption dominate your thinking, and you get lost.

Staying Jesus-focused also impacts the way you see people; it enables you to see them the way Jesus sees them. There is a tendency in this kind of work to divide the world into victims and abusers, to see the exploiters in the sex trafficking industry as the enemy. Pimps, madams, brothel owners, and corrupt officials become the objects of anger, hatred, and contempt.

Jesus never saw anyone or any group of people as the enemy. In fact, Jesus went out of His way to bring new life and transformation to the oppressor as well as the oppressed. He called a corrupt tax collector to be one of His disciples—while the man was extorting money from the poor (Luke 5:27). Jesus was called the "friend of tax collectors and sinners" (Matt. 11:19).

When a Roman army officer, the face of foreign oppression to the Jewish people, sent representatives to Jesus to request that Jesus heal his favorite slave, Jesus not only healed the slave, but also told His followers that He had never seen faith like that of the oppressor (Luke 7:9). Let that sink in for a moment. Jesus was telling God's chosen people that an uncircumcised Gentile, a member of an out-group, who did not order his life by Torah, was an exemplar of faith.

As Jesus hung dying on the cross, He lifted up His eyes to God the Father and prayed, "Father, forgive them; for they know not what they do" (Luke 23:34, KJV). Jesus was always clear about who the enemy was; the enemy was not a human or any group of humans. The enemy is Satan and his kingdom. The citizens of planet Earth may be bound or oppressed. They may be victim or oppressor. Jesus was clear about how He saw all of them when the religious leaders of the day criticized Him for identifying with the wrong crowd. He said, "It is not the healthy who need a doctor, but the sick. I have not come to call the righteous, but sinners" (Mark 2:17). Our outreach is to everyone, not just the victims. Everyone needs to be saved—the victim, the madam, the pimp, and the corrupt politician.

People often ask us and other team members the secret to Project Rescue's success and longevity. The answer is simple and profound: it is Jesus. Seeing people as Jesus sees them is the reason brothel owners, pimps, madams, and even corrupt police have come to Jesus in the cities where Project Rescue works.

2. We Offer Holistic Ministry

Project Rescue is committed to holistic ministry to the victims of sex trafficking because Jesus came to offer a whole salvation, not just a soul salvation. He ministered to people at every level. When they were hungry, He fed them. When they were sick, He healed them. When they were harassed by evil powers, He set them free. His teaching spoke to every aspect of their lives. Jesus Himself said as much when He spoke publicly the first time:

> The Spirit of the Lord is on me, because he has anointed me to proclaim good news to the poor. He has sent me to proclaim freedom for the prisoners and recovery of sight for the blind, to set the oppressed free, to proclaim the year of the Lord's favor.
>
> —Luke 4:18–19

Later, He told His first followers, "I have come that you might have life and have it more abundantly." (See John 10:10.)

At Project Rescue holistic ministry means we seek to minister grace and healing to every part of the person who has been fractured by sin—the mind, the heart, and the body. Holistic ministry recognizes that people are intricate, multidimensional beings and that every part of a woman, girl, or boy is damaged by sexual violence. The trauma of rape, physical abuse, and exploitation impacts every aspect of a young person's existence.

Holistic ministry is intense, one-on-one ministry. It cannot be done remotely and typically requires years to bring a young woman to health and wholeness. April Foster talks about the months required to gain a young woman's trust. It could easily take months before a young woman accepts an invitation to join her for tea or coffee at the Oasis outreach center. Devaraj reports that it sometimes takes two years before some women will even talk with him.

This does not mean evangelism is unimportant, but a holistic approach to ministry sets what we do in a context that is faithful to the way Jesus ministered to hurting people.

3. WE ENCOURAGE COLLABORATION AND PARTNERSHIPS

Despite the fact that God used Beth and I (David) to establish Project Rescue and carry the story around the world, the ministry has never been about us. Any telling of the Project Rescue story must begin with Devaraj and his team's outreach to the red-light district in Mumbai. It is also the story of my long friendship with Devaraj. Project Rescue has been a story of collaboration and partnership from the beginning. It is absolutely *not* the story of American heroes riding to the rescue of victims. It has always been about teams of believers, equal in every respect, working together in an atmosphere of love and mutual respect.

Leadership expert John Maxwell famously said, "If you want to do something big, you must link up with others. *One is too small a number to achieve greatness.*"[1] Project Rescue embodies that principle in every city where it has been established. Not all the team members working with Devaraj are staff members. Local police have often reached out to Project Rescue staff to take underage children out of the brothels and admit them to the children's home. The chief of police has been a firm friend of the ministry, as have madams and pimps in the red-light district who themselves were trafficked as children. Project Rescue leaders in several countries have forged effective and enduring working partnerships with local and national governments. Some Project Rescue initiatives have gained favor and funding from local governments.

One of the unexpected connections has been between Devaraj and the manager of the Hard Rock Cafe in his city, who routinely provides food for the women and children living in ministry homes. He has such a heart for the ministry that he presented the need to Hamish Dodds, the president of Hard Rock International, who made a significant donation to build a vocational training center and produced a coffee table book about the ministry to help raise funds.

Project Rescue has benefited from partnerships with ministries and missionaries around the world. Chair of the Bombay Teen Challenge board for twenty-eight years, Dr. Ivan Satyavrata, pointedly and succinctly states, "Project Rescue sees itself primarily as a network rather than as an organization."

Satyavrata has a unique vantage point. In addition to being the chairman of the Project Rescue board and continuing to serve on the Bombay Teen Challenge board, he is a member of the World Vision International board, an adjunct faculty member at Assemblies of God Theological Seminary, a former president of Southern Asia Bible College, and CEO of the ministries in Kolkata established by missionary pioneer Mark Buntain. He once observed that cooperation is in the ministry's DNA. "Collaboration has been the secret to [Project Rescue's] success," he said. "It is second nature to David and Beth Grant."[2] Satyavrata knows that Beth and I spent thirty years in collaborative relationships and partnerships before launching Project Rescue. It is who we are.

Collaboration is much more than a buzzword; it goes to the heart of what it means to be kingdom-minded, and it is how the kingdom advances. Jesus told His disciples, "If two of you on earth agree about anything they ask for, it will be done for them by my Father in heaven. For where two or three gather in my name, there am I with them" (Matt. 18:19–20). Jesus could not have stated the matter with greater clarity: unity, collaboration, and partnership are not luxuries; they are the essence of God's kingdom and the means for maximizing the liberating power of the gospel.

The heart of collaboration is shared vision and life, even as it was to the first Jesus followers (Acts 2:42–47). If collaboration is a biblical imperative, it is also a practical necessity. Project Rescue leaders have recognized that there is simply no way to tackle a web of evil so vast, intricate, and entrenched without the collaboration of ministries, nonprofit organizations, and civic and business leaders. That is at the heart of the Project Rescue story.

4. WE ARE SPIRIT-EMPOWERED

I (Beth) am firm on this point: You don't get transformation without Spirit empowerment. (See my article in Appendix A, "In Step With the Spirit," for more about this.) This is true everywhere but especially in South Asia, where the structure of sexual slavery is a complex interaction of hierarchy, social class, gender roles, and customs. But operating parallel to and insidiously intertwined with culture is a dark spiritual world where the real struggle occurs. Paul stated this forcefully to a group of new believers in the city of Ephesus: "For our struggle is not against flesh and blood, but against the rulers, against the authorities, against the powers of this dark world and against the spiritual forces of evil in the heavenly realms" (Eph. 6:12).

This evil does not yield itself to programs, politics, or advocacy, however well-intentioned they may be. Westerners have difficulty understanding this given the way the supernatural has been pushed to the margins of Western life and education. Added to this, the American experience of building a new nation makes it difficult for us to understand the depth and strength of entrenched social systems or the hold that centuries of tradition have on people, even in church. Believers from South Asia and Africa grasp this intuitively, as all ministry in those regions is viewed as part of the battle between good and evil. One Project Rescue leader talks about villages in his nation where families have trafficked their daughters for more than five hundred years. The unjust chains of custom and class are not broken by good intentions.

Being Spirit-empowered for ministry was a lesson Jesus' first followers also had to learn. When Jesus' disciples struggled to bring deliverance to a child tormented by evil spirits, Jesus told them plainly, "This kind can come out by nothing but prayer and fasting" (Mark 9:29, NKJV). When you invade the spiritual world, human effort cannot get the job done. Followers of Jesus must have kingdom power to set captives free.

Millions of Jesus followers around the world have

discovered that the gateway to such power comes through the baptism in the Holy Spirit, an experience analogous to being immersed in water (indicated by the Greek *baptizo*) that ushered the first believers into the fullness of the Holy Spirit's presence, power, and prophetic witness. The narrative arc of the Book of Acts is the story of God taking people to places they had never been to do things they had never done, of ordinary people doing extraordinary things. That is the story of Project Rescue. Some of the most effective staff in Project Rescue ministry centers are women who themselves were prostituted or born into brothels. They have been saved, healed, and delivered from dark powers and learned to become channels of the same power that changed their lives.

5. WE ARE CHURCH-BASED

From the start, Devaraj organized the women and children reached through the ministry to the red-light district into local groups of believers. That loving, supportive community has provided a place of safety and nurture for these wounded women. It is what the New Testament calls church, and it is an essential foundation stone for Project Rescue.

In his letter to the Corinthians the apostle Paul wrote to what was then a new group of Jesus followers and described what happened to them in radical terms. He stated that they were "new creations" for whom "old things have passed away; behold, all things have become new" (2 Cor. 5:17, NKJV). He told another group they were now "fellow citizens," members of "[God's] household" (Eph. 2:19–20). Paul also reminded the group of fractious, highly individualistic Greeks in Corinth that they were "the body of Christ" (1 Cor. 12:27).

Those are stunning new realities and liberating truth. Understanding and learning to live in this power is not something that happens automatically, especially for those whose very identities have been distorted by sexual exploitation and its lies. The new Jesus follower has a lot to learn and even more to unlearn. That is why Paul wrote most of his letters to these groups of Jesus followers and why he devoted so much energy to establishing, nurturing, and encouraging these new believers.

The process is similar to moving to a foreign country. Many of us who work with Project Rescue have spent a great deal of time living and working outside the cultures of our birth. When we relocated from our birth culture, we had to learn a new language, learn how to use different currencies, and adapt to the customs and culture of our new home. No matter who we were at home—how educated we were or how accomplished we may have been—we had a lot to learn to live in and minister to our new world. If you think of church as a group of people gathered to learn how to love and live like Jesus, then you will know why it is so important.

The idea of church as a community and family of faith may seem outdated. Part of the reason is that for centuries church in the West has been a place you go instead of a group of redeemed people who join together to learn how to follow Jesus, encourage one another, and work together to share hope with others. If church in the red-light district had been merely a place to go, it would have failed. The church in the red-light district was a lifeline to the trafficked women and their children, a source of hope, caring, and support. It became their family.

Cultural concepts about church come and go, but the idea of a people unified in Christ, empowered by the Holy Spirit, and living in community with one another is the heart of the gospel. The church is a community of hope that extends the love, grace, and healing of Jesus to those without hope and welcomes them to belong as they pursue Jesus and their journey to freedom.

One more critical point must be made about the church-based character of Project Rescue. Project Rescue would not exist without the prayers, encouragement, counsel, and support of the church. Some ministries call themselves "parachurch," which means they operate apart from the church. Many of these ministries were founded by enormously gifted spiritual entrepreneurs who lived in a world apart from the church. They might "go to church" or even be church members, but at their core what they do and who they are is apart from the church.

Since the Second World War this approach to ministry has launched thousands of evangelistic and compassion ministries in every part of the world. Some of their accomplishments have been impressive. They have moved with energy, agility, and creativity. However, the lack of church involvement has also resulted in a lack of accountability among leaders and a lack of relational connection that has often had tragic results for leaders, their families, and the people they lead.

The leaders and team members of Project Rescue are part of Christ's universal body of believers and members of local congregations. They live in fellowship and accountability with others and benefit daily from the gifts and graces operating in those local families of faith.

This young Muslim woman living in Europe represents just one of the many people groups Project Rescue ministers to in red-light districts such as the ones shown here in South Asia and Europe.

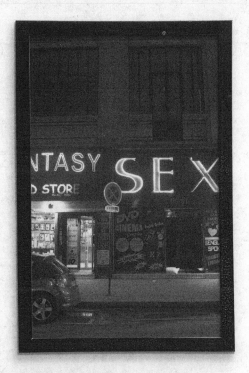

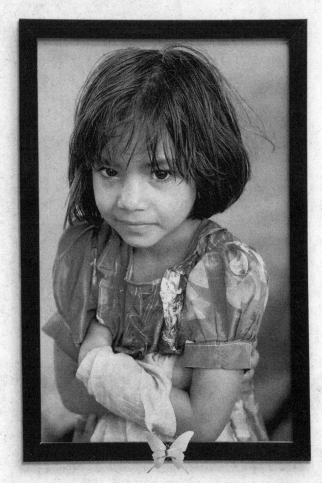

Children of the red-light district see, hear, and
experience things no child ever should.

Project Rescue offers hope for a better future not only to women in the red-light districts but also to their children.

These young girls are catching up after their school day in a Project Rescue aftercare home in South Asia.

Giving girls an opportunity to go to school is part of Project Rescue's holistic approach to ministry, which aims to reach the whole person—mind, heart, and body.

More than anything, Project Rescue aftercare homes, such as these in Europe and South Asia, provide a sense of belonging to a family.

A young woman has devotional time at a Project
Rescue aftercare home in South Asia.

Prayer and Bible study at Project Rescue aftercare
homes play a critical role in transforming the lives of
the young women and girls the ministry reaches.

A young girl dances outside a Project Rescue
aftercare home in South Asia.

ABOVE: This young woman (center) is a sex trafficking survivor who now works with Project Rescue in Europe. BELOW: Project Rescue aftercare homes are filled with fun activities such as learning dance routines.

From making jewelry to sewing brightly colored clothing, vocational training teaches women how to make an independent living so they never have to return to the horrors of the red-light districts.

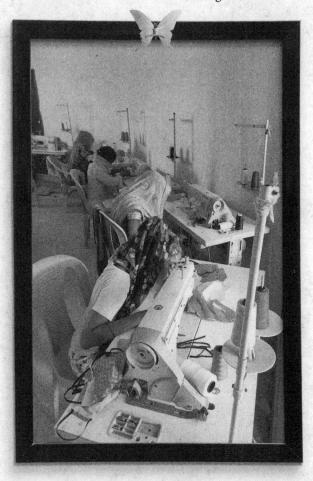

Twenty-five years ago Sonu, Sumi, Priya, and Pinky were among the first young girls rescued from a red-light district in South Asia. They grew up in a Project Rescue aftercare home—and bonded like sisters. All four young women have now completed college and are pursuing careers they're passionate about. Sonu works as an arts and crafts schoolteacher, Sumi is an educational adviser at a center for overseas educational management, Priya is employed as a financial analyst, and Pinky is an executive at a large company in South Asia. We celebrate what God has done in the lives of these young women and many others!

 Not only does vocational training help women escape red-light districts; it also sets their children on a new path.

Children are free to be children once they are rescued and restored from the horrors of the red-light district. Project Rescue has ministered to thousands of children like these little girls over the last twenty-five years.

For every woman rescued from sexual slavery, often
a little child is rescued too.

This woman, walking with her child, represents the many women and children being ministered to through Project Rescue outreach programs in Europe.

A young girl plays at a Project Rescue aftercare home in South Asia. When a child feels safe and loved, it shows.

Jesus: the reason and motivation for everything
we do!

Chapter 6

PROJECT RESCUE 2.0

PROJECT RESCUE IS not a multinational company, franchise, or brand; it helps launch, support, and facilitate ministries to victims of sex trafficking around the world. For fifteen years after the first initiative, the ministry concentrated its efforts on three nations in South Asia and the God-given dream of liberating the one million children enslaved by sex trafficking. Partnering with friends, nonprofit organizations, and governments, in the first fifteen years we established homes for trafficked women and children brought out of the red-light districts, as well as vocational training centers.

Every initiative carried the same DNA—the outgoing love of God for those whose lives had been devastated by sexual exploitation expressed through rescue, restoration, and prevention. Despite similarities, every initiative was as unique as the persons God used to do the work and the doors He opened to them.

Sometimes, ministry leaders are people who were

influenced by me (Beth) or David during their student days, when God planted the seed in their heart that grew into a life calling. Lisa Russi took my class in intercultural ministry while she was enrolled at Evangel University in Springfield, Missouri. She told me she wanted to work with me someday. Shortly after graduating from Evangel, Lisa went to a city in South Asia, where she pioneered a Project Rescue outreach in 2003.

The initiative in one major city of South Asia began serendipitously. It was not the result of any grand strategy; our colleague Lucy Donaldson was just there to help her friend Vinita Bhalla, who had worked with Lucy and her husband, Kevin, to start a school in the 1990s.

Our oldest daughter, Rebecca, and a national worker had begun visiting the red-light district, which has been the center of prostitution in the city for more than six hundred years. They had been told it was impossible to do any ministry there. But they began getting to know mothers and their children. Vinita learned of that fledgling initiative and later took into her home a young woman who had been rescued from the brothel. Soon several young girls from the red-light district were living in her home, each one a breakthrough. When the Donaldsons returned in 2010, Vinita took Lucy to the red-light district.

More than a thousand girls and young women work the narrow street near the railroad station, many of them brought there from rural villages in the north by boyfriends who tricked them with promises of a better life. The procurer would marry the girl and then put her on a train for the city. Upon arrival, he would take her off the train and throw her into a brothel, where she would be systematically beaten and raped. The pimps can break most girls in seventy-two hours. She will never resist again.

The trafficked women would often look at Vinita or Lucy and say, "It's too late for me. But can you do something for my child?"

Vinita and Lucy knew they had to do something. They learned that if they didn't get a child out of a brothel by age eleven, she would end up working in the brothel. The boys would also have begun working, first as "tea boys," who would fetch tea for the customers. Then when they got older, they would become procurers.

Vinita and Lucy realized they needed a safe place where the women and their children could visit, receive prayer, or just watch TV. They rented a little upstairs flat in the heart of the red-light district. Within two years Project Rescue owned the building. A local doctor started an open clinic because the hospital would not take the girls from the district.

Something seismic was occurring deep in the hearts of a newly emerging group of courageous women and men to extend the ministry of Jesus to those in bondage in other parts of the world.

Come Over and Help Us

Project Rescue went to Europe in response to appeals for help, the first triggered by a meeting between me (Beth) and Fiona Bellshaw in 2011. Fiona is the daughter of Salvation Army missionaries in Argentina. Her father graduated from university and became a social worker. Her parents took the words of Jesus in Matthew 25 literally to "feed the hungry and clothe the naked." They took refugees from Chile and Uganda into their home. From early childhood, Fiona grew up around people who did not have a protected life as she did.

When Fiona was young, her parents went to a Pentecostal church where they received the baptism in the Holy Spirit. For each of them, it was a baptism in compassion. Her father started bringing homeless people into their house. It fostered understanding and empathy in Fiona.

Fiona's father felt called to Spain. No one could have known that Spain would become home. Fiona married Juan Carlos Escobar, a Spanish pastor, and the couple planted churches, mainly in Barcelona. For the next couple of decades, Fiona did all the things a pastor's wife does. There was nothing extraordinary about her life. Toward midlife, Fiona began to feel there was something more for her to do, which was strange because she had been sick for six or seven years with a degenerative disease. She had problems with her blood, skin, and muscles. She did not get better. During this time, God dealt with her in a deeper way. Her own experience of suffering produced a compassion in her she had not known.

An event occurred in 2001 that changed Fiona's life and ministry. A trafficked woman from South America came to their church and committed her life to Christ. From that time, God began to bring trafficked women to Fiona. In 2004 Fiona and her husband moved to Madrid, where she took a course on human trafficking. She and her husband were working with some missionaries, who told her that she needed to meet me (Beth). Later, Fiona attended an event in Lyon, France, where we finally met. At a subsequent world congress of leaders hosted by her denomination in 2011, Fiona met with me and other Project Rescue leaders.

Fiona told me, "I want to be part of Project Rescue." She keenly felt a need for mentoring.

The ministry in Spain carries the same DNA as the original initiative. It is based on the aftercare approach in which survivors live in a home and become family. Despite any cultural differences, the spiritual, physical, and emotional devastation in the life of a woman or girl is the same.

Just like the first initiatives of Project Rescue, the approach in each of the homes in Spain is holistic. In addition to the basic needs of shelter, food, and safety, every woman is cared for medically and psychologically because of the trauma she has suffered.

Project Rescue offers legal help through its legal arm, Solidarity, which provides advocacy in the courts.

The initiative in Spain is also church-based. Fiona and her teams do not go into an area without a commitment from a local church to support the outreach. Some of those churches are small, but they provide a spiritual nursery where new believers come to know Jesus and become part of a body of believers.

Despite the similarities, there are profound differences between the initiatives in Madrid and South Asia. The population of trafficked women and girls in Madrid is far more diverse. The Project Rescue team ministers to victims from at least sixty countries, most of whom do not speak Spanish. Many, like Adanna, come from Africa. Like Adanna, they have been brought to the country on fake passports.

Relations with governments present special challenges in Spain and throughout the European Union. Activities that operate in the private sector in the United States are under much closer government scrutiny in Europe. In Spain, as in most European countries, a ministry such as Project Rescue must register with the government. Its activities are routinely audited. In those early years, Fiona made contacts with local and national authorities to understand their needs and vision.

Fiona and her team have discovered that one of the main problems in Spain is that prostitution and the sexual exploitation of women has been deeply embedded in the culture over centuries. There is also the lie that women choose this life. In addition, there are mafias in each city. The mafia makes no less than five million euros a day in Spain from sex trafficking, making it the fastest-growing activity in Europe. Girls leaving the life are a threat to business, and if the mafia excels at one thing, it is protecting their interests by any means necessary.

Because of this, the women and girls in Project Rescue homes are protected by the government as part of witness protection. Project Rescue has no visibility or social profile in Europe as it does in the United States.

Fiona's strategy works. The government has been supportive of Project Rescue, even to the extent of providing significant financial support for the homes. By 2021, Project Rescue had expanded to seven cities in Spain. And Spain is where a young woman named Isabella found hope after being trapped in the sex trade.

No Longer Hopeless

Isabella was lost in her thoughts, overwhelmed with the situation she found herself in. Blessed with two children but having no income, she struggled to make ends meet and provide for her children. Her thoughts drifted to her sister, who lived in Spain; by all appearances, life seemed to be going well for her.

Isabella's thoughts seemed to spiral every day, leading her to the same decision: "If I move to Spain, I can make a better life for me and my children." So she packed up a few of her belongings, left her children with her mother, and tearfully said goodbye as she set off for Spain.

Upon arriving, Isabella discovered the harsh reality that her sister's "job" was prostitution. Bewildered and disheartened, Isabella left her sister in search of other options by which to survive. However, since she had only recently arrived in Spain, she had no other contacts besides her sister, and she was left without a choice but to return to her sister to accept the "job offer."

As her sister took her to a store to buy the sexy clothes she needed to start the job, a sense of helplessness overwhelmed her. Feeling ashamed and deceived, yet thinking she had no other choice, Isabella began to "work." Time passed until COVID-19 began flooding the news. Everything shut down, including the club where Isabella worked, and she was forced to move to a twenty-four-hour apartment, a type of housing in Spain that is used solely for prostitution.

It was at this apartment that Isabella met the "We Hear Your Voice" detection team, who intuitively knew she was being prostituted against her will. Initially, she was fearful to accept their help. However, the team continued to reach out while building trust and giving Isabella "Bags of Hope" filled with food and hygiene products. Eventually Isabella made the decision to accept a place at one of the team's safe homes.

Today Isabella continues on a healing journey, and

her bubbly, lively, and fun-loving spirit is shining through. Her determination to do well drives her as she excels in cooking and baking. She is currently taking a hairdressing course as well. God is resurrecting His hope within her. No longer helpless and hopeless, Isabella looks to the future with hope and expectation, believing that with God's help and ours, she will make a beautiful home for herself and her children.

Western Europe

Northern Europe presents different challenges. The sex trade is legal in the Netherlands and operates in a gray zone of tolerance in a number of other countries. Hundreds of thousands of young women from Eastern and Southern Europe, Africa, and South America have been trafficked to the region. But "where sin increased, grace increased all the more" (Rom. 5:20). Assemblies of God missions executive Paul Trementozzi told me (Beth) that so many new missionaries were coming to Europe saying, "God has given me a heart for trafficked women," that Paul and his team wanted to give the emerging group of leaders training and a track to run on.[1] They also wanted to ensure that the next generation would have the biblical, missiological, and practical knowledge needed to avoid making costly mistakes that could endanger the ministry and the lives of the women and girls God called them to serve.

April Foster and Shawn Alderman represent the

wave of leaders God has brought to Europe. April and her husband moved to Belgium in 2001. April had been hearing about trafficking for a couple of years. In 2007, she decided to visit the city's red-light district and was appalled to see young women literally displayed 24/7 in over two hundred windows in the area. Men came from around the world to "window shop" for women from fifty countries. There was something for every taste.

April did not know where to start, so she invited a colleague, Drue Huffman, to start doing prayer walks with her in the district. She felt impressed to give flowers to the girls in the windows. The flowers opened the door. Later, another colleague, Shawn Alderman, started passing out coffee and tea. You do not find much trust in human nature in a red-light district. The young women in the windows were understandably reluctant. They wanted to know why the two women were there. Shawn first went to the red-light district on a Friday night. They told her to come at a less busy time. Little by little, April and Shawn built friendships. They soon realized they needed a different setting for sharing, prayer, counseling, and Bible studies. The Oasis Center opened in 2010. Once the women had their own place, they opened up and shared their stories.

One question kept coming up, no matter where a woman came from: "Jesus loves me, but how does that change my situation?"

The women needed help with language and legal

problems. The Oasis Center soon became a resource to the women of the red-light district. The women also needed a church home. April and her husband chose Christian Center in Brussels as a church family for themselves and the women. The church embraced and supported the work. So did Continental Theological Seminary, which provided interns and regularly sent ministry teams to Antwerp.

Her success made her a valuable resource throughout Europe, and she began training and mentoring leaders.

Lisa Russi moved to Grenoble, France, to work as part of a church-planting team and started a street outreach among prostituted women. As in many European cities, immigrant women there from Eastern Europe and Nigeria suffer the most from sexual exploitation. French pastors in other parts of France had already been ministering to the sexually exploited, which opened the door for Lisa's ministry. Evangelical churches and ministries in Grenoble have embraced the outreach there. They pray and supply volunteers.

Paul Trementozzi, the administrator responsible for coordinating the efforts of the US Assemblies of God in Europe, and his team had witnessed the impact of Project Rescue throughout South Asia. They believed Assemblies of God personnel in Europe who wanted to work with trafficked women and children would benefit by affiliating with Project Rescue.

David and I (Beth) had focused our efforts on the doors God opened in South Asia, which had been our passion and burden for decades. But here was an opportunity to hold up the hands of men and women with the same vision and heart we had. The opportunity also underscored the potential of unified action in the face of evil. The people God has called to "set the oppressed free" (Luke 4:18) will be stronger and more effective together. In these partnerships, no one loses identity, but everyone finds resources and support for what God has called them to do.

OPEN DOORS IN POST-CHRISTIAN EUROPE

Most of the nations of Northern Europe have been secular for generations, certainly since the 1920s when the generation coming out of the First World War rejected Christianity as being anti-modern. Most government leaders have a bias against faith-based ministries and see little or no place for them in postmodern Europe, except the place the state allows them to have. As nations from Southern and Eastern Europe have been incorporated into the European community, the secularist mentality has actively pushed all expressions of religion to the margins of society. Religion is a problem to be managed or eliminated, not an instrument for good.

There is also the difference in the religious worldviews of the women who come to Project Rescue homes. Because so few Europeans observe any religion, many of the women we serve know very little about Jesus. Project Rescue team members introduce women to Christ by demonstrating His love. Many discover the transforming power of that love. For some, like Adanna, who had learned about Jesus in her church in Africa, the journey is a short one. For others, it takes months or even years. Despite the formidable challenges, Project Rescue has touched the lives of hundreds of young women across Europe.

Project Rescue leaders in Europe see the continent's post-Christian mindset as an opportunity instead of a threat. Fiona Bellshaw states the case powerfully: "I believe the church is here to be a light, and to be that light we have to get out of our mentality of only speaking to or working with Christians. If we had only done that, we could not have done most of what we have done." She urges a strategy that will work almost anyplace in the world: "We have to open the circle. There are many people who are not followers of Jesus but who share the vision to end trafficking."[2]

When building relationships with the government, no matter what level of government she works with, Fiona always starts with one question: "How can we help you?" No matter where she or Project Rescue teams in Spain have gone, they ask to meet the person responsible for the victims of sex trafficking. They also ask to meet the mayor, the police, the leaders of the Institute for Women, and the directors of social services.

The success speaks for itself: Project Rescue now works in seven of Spain's seventeen autonomous regions. Project Rescue Spain has also become a part of the National Network Against Human Trafficking, an umbrella including Amnesty International and the Red Cross, as well as specialized organizations focused on sex trafficking. And in a development no one would have imagined twenty years ago, Project Rescue requested and now receives financial support from a number of Spanish government ministries both at the local and national levels.

TRAINING THE TRAINERS

A hallmark of the last decade has been a rising commitment to resource the men and women God calls to minister freedom and grace to the victims of sex trafficking. Much of this is relational. Often Project Rescue leaders from different regions meet virtually to encourage each other, strategize, share needs, and pray for one another.

Training new leaders and providing ongoing training and support for experienced leaders has become integral to the ministry of Project Rescue. Some years ago, on behalf of the Faith Alliance Against Slavery and Trafficking (FAAST), of which Project Rescue was a founding member, I (Beth) led a team of more than forty evangelical writers to develop an introductory curriculum for people involved in providing transformational aftercare to victims of sexual exploitation. Many people have taken the Hands That Heal course since the book was first published in 2007.

Church and ministry leaders need more in-depth training in how to minister to the victims of sexual exploitation and help their churches become places of healing for victims. To assist with this, a team of Project Rescue leaders, counselors, practitioners, and I designed six college-level certificate courses covering key aspects of this specialized ministry. The six-course program is called Rescue & Restore, and almost one hundred students from nineteen countries participated in the first year of the program.

Over the years we have increasingly focused on providing this kind of high-level training. Across twenty-five years of coleading Project Rescue with David, I have been privileged to speak to thousands internationally on the subject of sex trafficking and how churches can provide healing and Jesus-centered ministry to victims. I have also taught on college and university campuses in the United States, Europe, and India, where young people have been inspired to commit their lives to the ministry of setting captives free.

Project Rescue has certainly not been alone in this effort. A number of universities and seminaries have added courses on trafficking to their curricula. Lisa Russi now teaches at Northwest University in Kirkland, Washington, where Joe Castleberry, EdD, a longtime friend of Project Rescue, is president. Dr. Castleberry's commitment to equip the next generation of women and men who will minister to the victims of sexual exploitation means training has become part of Northwest's course offerings. The work with institutions of higher education has fostered an informal coalition with professors and administrators who have a heart for the victims.

As important and life-changing as the work in the red-light districts of the world has been, perhaps training the trainers is one of the most strategic aspects of Project Rescue's ministry today.

Toward Sustainability

For several hundred years the model for raising funds for ministries like Project Rescue has been based on making direct appeals to friends and supporters. This approach propelled the efforts of the modern missions movement, enabling it to take the gospel to every corner of the world. But this strategy is heavily dependent on the personalities and appeal of the mission. Often it breaks down when the founder passes off the scene.

David and I (Beth) felt compelled to move Project Rescue toward a more sustainable model. Under the entrepreneurial leadership of our son-in-law Jonathan Barratt, the Project Rescue Foundation was launched in 2013 to develop nontraditional revenue streams to defray operational costs and fund projects.

Through planned giving, corporate sponsorships, and general appeals beyond the church world, the foundation has raised more than twelve million dollars since its inception. It also provides a vehicle that enables US leaders to become personally engaged in bringing freedom and healing to the victims of sex trafficking.

The foundation sponsors events where pastors and other leaders gather to connect, learn more about what God is doing through Project Rescue, discover how to carry the fight for freedom to their own communities, and build a network of friends and support.

The foundation also provides a vehicle for business leaders and professionals to become personally engaged. Tim Wegner connected with Project Rescue Foundation at one of these events and has become a powerful example of what one person can do. Tim had recently stepped off the board of another organization and had been praying that God would define his next steps. Upon hearing about the foundation, he felt compelled to get involved, telling Jonathan, "I'm all in; Project Rescue has the next twenty years of my life."[3] Tim became one of the foundation's leading financial supporters. Not long after that, Tim joined the board of Project Rescue Foundation and has since moved into the role of board chairman.

Tim has become an advocate for Project Rescue and a catalyst to engage businesspeople. His efforts have led to millions of dollars flowing into Project Rescue Foundation. Tim's wife, Mindy, also advocates for Project Rescue. A trained communicator and executive leadership coach, she has provided training and education for Project Rescue staff and leaders. Tim's sister and brother-in-law, Cindee and Mark Heath, also caught the heart and vision behind Project

Rescue. They have become generous supporters, and Cindee has joined the board of Project Rescue. These two couples have been grafted into the Project Rescue family and are using their connections, influence, and resources to make an exponential impact on the outreach. Most importantly, they are impacting the lives of the women and children Project Rescue serves.

Chapter 7

WOUNDED HEALERS

T HE MINISTRY OF Project Rescue aims at nothing less than restoring the image of God in the lives of those whose bodies and psyches have been shattered by torture and abuse. It is about helping sexually violated women and children discover their identity, health, and dignity as daughters and sons of God.

It takes a special person to minister healing to sexually violated young women and their children. While Project Rescue team leaders are highly gifted people, it is not their giftedness alone that makes them effective, though it certainly helps them to frame difficult issues, envision creative solutions, and devise effective strategies. But where it matters most—on the streets of the red-light districts across our world—the key qualification for effective ministry is an authentic identification with brokenness.

More than a generation ago, Henri Nouwen, a professor of spirituality at Harvard University, urged a new vision of Christian ministry. He wrote, "How can we put our woundedness in the service of others? When our wounds cease to be a source of shame, and become a source of healing, we have become wounded healers."[1] These "wounded healers" are men and women who themselves had been broken by life but who experienced the healing grace of God. Nouwen believed that only those who have been broken and found healing could identify with the hurting and minister God's grace to them

Many of the workers in Project Rescue homes and ministry centers are like Amy, who now works in the ministry in Madrid. Amy was born into grinding poverty in Nigeria, and like millions of other African girls she imagined Europe as an escape, a place where she could find work and happiness. As it was with Adanna, traffickers promised Amy's family that she would become a nanny to a wealthy family in Spain. When she arrived, she found herself in an alternate reality. When Amy protested, the traffickers told her they would kill her and her family if she tried to escape. When she came to Project Rescue's Home of Hope, every level of Amy's life had been destroyed. After months of restorative ministry, Amy became healthy, happy, and motivated to help others. Today she is one of our counselors.

Even those who have not suffered the horrors of trafficking have dealt with the brokenness of loss, sickness, depression, deep hurt, and loneliness. They have experienced God's healing and learned how to let God use them to bring healing to others. The compassion built into Fiona Bellshaw by her experience of sickness and suffering would be rare for a person who had not lived through a similar experience. I (Beth) became a widow at the age of twenty-five. Every member of the Project Rescue team has been wounded and broken and then experienced healing in some way. Take Mather, for instance.

Shining Light in Darkness

When Mather was nineteen, an Italian businessman came to her village in Kenya speaking of a better, more prosperous life on the European continent. Mather was lured to leave the beauty of her country for empty promises. She followed the businessman to Italy, where the man suddenly took her into his own home to live as his "wife," though he never made it official. After bearing a son, she pleaded with him to officially marry her, but he refused.

Years passed, and as Mather aged she fell sick and underwent needed surgeries. A new fear set in when she discovered that this man had replaced her by marrying a younger woman from the African continent, and she suddenly found herself thrown out and living on the streets. Without legal residency in Italy or opportunities in her home country, she accepted an invitation from a Muslim businessman to work in Finland. After arriving, she quickly realized the serious danger she was in when the Muslim businessman began threatening her and forcing her to deliver drugs for his drug-trafficking business.

Feeling desperate for a way out, she convinced the man to allow her to leave the house and made her way to a local social services office. Burdened by her story, they contacted the police and formed a plan for her escape. She returned to the home, and while she was frantically packing her belongings, the front door opened and the man walked in. As dread and fear set in, she heard the sirens in the distance as the police came to rescue her and put an end to the nightmare she was trapped in. A wave of relief washed over her as she was placed in a temporary shelter, but it was short-lived. The weight of all the broken promises and shattered hopes and dreams broke Mather from the inside out.

Later that week, Maureen, a Finnish citizen who was born and raised in Kenya, arrived and took Mather to a Project Rescue aftercare home. As Maureen entered the home, she prayed words of hope and healing over Mather. Mather felt the Holy Spirit rush over her; she realized Maureen was praying in her mother tongue and began to weep. This marked the beginning of Mather's healing journey, and thankfully it did not end there.

Her heart is deeply burdened to minister to others who are trapped in similar situations as hers. She knows the pain and understands the fear and feelings of helplessness. In following this call on her life, she has been trained by leaders in the aftercare home and is now a vital part of the ministry team. As the Lord pieces together Mather's own shattered dreams, He is using her to shine a light into places where it feels all other lights have gone out.

QUALIFIED BY SUFFERING

The model for the wounded healer is our Lord Himself, who "was wounded for our transgressions, he was bruised for our iniquities: the chastisement of our peace was upon him; and with his stripes we are healed" (Isa. 53:5, KJV). Jesus took the sickness and sorrow of the world into His own person. He did not hold the hurting at a distance; He took their sickness and woundedness into His own soul. This is what Project Rescue team members do. It is what those who minister effectively have always done. They have learned that God's strength is made perfect in our weakness— not in our strength. (See 2 Corinthians 12:9.)

This is not the prevailing model of ministry in a world where talent and charisma count for more than suffering, where many ministers model themselves after CEOs, motivational speakers, and celebrities. And yet the writer of Hebrews states that it was suffering that qualified Jesus to be our High Priest: "For this reason he had to be made like them, fully human in every way, in order that he might become a merciful and faithful high priest in service to God, and that he might make atonement for the sins of the people" (Heb. 2:17).

Jesus knew what it was to suffer pain, disgrace, and humiliation. He was part of a despised, largely impoverished minority group in a world where Roman power and Greek wisdom were pinnacles of human achievement. The writer of Hebrews states clearly that it was suffering that enabled Jesus to fulfill His priestly ministry. And it is their genuine personal identification with suffering and healing that enables Project Rescue team members to be channels of God's grace and healing.

Consider Sonia's story.

RENEWED HOPE

Sonia sat wringing her hands as she looked around her single bedroom home, ashamed of the life she found herself living. Servicing customers had become the only life she knew. Her life was a trail of false promises, bitter betrayals, and shattered dreams.

It had not always been like this. For a brief moment in time, she was an innocent little girl with a bright future ahead. Yet this was stripped from her when her mother suddenly died. Her father quickly remarried a woman who seemed to look for every opportunity to inflict pain. She withdrew Sonia from school, deprived her of food, and physically and verbally abused her.

At only thirteen years old, Sonia felt she had no other choice than to run away. On her journey, she met a woman who accepted her, took her in, and treated her in a way she always longed for since her mother died.

She began calling her "Mom," and for the first time in many years she felt loved. But one day Sonia learned the bitter truth—the woman's "love" for her was all a lie. She had simply been waiting for the right time to sell Sonia into prostitution. Confused, blindsided, and devastated, Sonia entered a living hell.

Days turned into months, and slowly the months turned into a year. Time eroded her hope to escape, and just when she was about to give up, one of her customers promised to help her escape after hearing her story. In the middle of the night, they fled and she began to hope for a future she had never imagined for herself. However, her hope was short-lived, as the man was suddenly arrested for unknown reasons, leaving her stranded, homeless, and without a way to support herself.

A wave of dread washed over her as she gathered her meager possessions. She realized she needed to find the only person in the city she knew—the woman who sold her, the woman she once thought loved her and whom she called Mom. The rest was a blur. Weary and exhausted, she found the woman, who took her in, yet not without a cost. Once again Sonia was forced to sell her body. And for the years that followed, she lived in this cyclical hell, feeling shamed by the lustful and degrading eyes of men and the abuse of those who physically beat her. Every day seemed to be a continuation of yesterday's pain.

For a moment she hoped life would change when she met a man who proposed and married her. But this proved to be another shattered dream, as after marriage her life in the sex trade continued. Betrayal and hurt continued when, not long afterward, a woman close to Sonia seized the opportunity and trafficked her into a different country, selling her to a brothel. After eight long months of trying to block out the haunting sounds and memories of the brothel, Sonia finally escaped and found her way back "home," where she met our Project Rescue team. "I've always wanted to live a good life and do good things with my life. I just never had the opportunity to do so," Sonia explained tearfully.

We met Sonia while pioneering a new Project Rescue ministry, and within a few days of sharing our vision with her, she unofficially took on the responsibilities of an outreach worker, going to her fellow "sisters" in the sex trade and offering them a way out through Project Rescue. At the time of this writing, Sonia has brought more than forty prostituted women into our program. She is a beacon of hope, helping to pave the way for other women and girls to come out of the trade. On the same streets where she used to walk as a sex worker, being harassed and treated as nothing, she is now shown respect; she walks with dignity. Her life has been a story of sorrow and tragedy, but God is showing her that He holds the pen and is rewriting it as a story of hope and promise. And what God has done for Sonia, He is doing for so many others.

Bravery in the Face of Danger

Over fourteen years ago, two young girls, Saanvi and Riya, were rescued from slavery and brought to a Project Rescue home. There they embarked on the journey to restoration and found healing and new life through Jesus Christ. They earned their degrees in counseling and caregiving and have since reintegrated into society.

Recently, the government asked Saanvi and Riya to assist in a rescue operation. Nervous that memories would resurface as a result of this operation, the young women hesitated at first but agreed to help. Their desire to see others experience the same freedom they now had outweighed their fear.

Despite their hearts racing and plaguing doubts, Saanvi and Riya walked into the room confidently as the police raided the motel they suspected of harboring trafficking. Their role was to convince the frightened young women and children to come with the police and to provide them comfort and compassion during a very uncertain and traumatic time.

Just as the police were finishing and preparing to leave, the memory of Riya's rescue flooded Saanvi's mind, and she remembered hiding under the bed until the police found her. She quickly spoke up and insisted they search under all the beds. As they searched, they found one last young girl.

While walking out of the motel, Saanvi and Riya counted the number of women rescued. They praised

God that because they were able to face their past and set aside their own memories, they could help bring thirty young girls into a life of freedom. They walked up to the officer in charge and asked, "So when is the next rescue scheduled?"

We rejoice with these two young women from our Project Rescue program as they help others find freedom—tangibly and boldly.

Chapter 8

MYSTERIES AND MIRACLES

AS WE THINK back over the twenty-five years of Project Rescue's ministry in South Asia and Europe, so many stirring miracles come to mind. The first comes from the earliest days of the ministry when more than one hundred women responded to Devaraj's message of hope when they heard it the first time.

Then there was the response of Nepali church leaders in Kathmandu when Devaraj challenged them with the story of Nepali girls who had been trafficked into Mumbai's red-light districts. After being rescued and brought to a safe Home of Hope for restoration, many of them asked Devaraj, "Uncle, can we go home?" Given the stigma and shame attached to prostitution in all of South Asia and the fact that many of them were HIV-positive, Devaraj felt he had to travel to Nepal and ask church leaders personally if indeed the girls could come home to Nepal. As Devaraj passionately shared, the assembled church leaders wept. Then he challenged them, "Is there room in your hearts and churches for Nepal's daughters? What do I tell them? Can they come home?"

With tears, church leaders said, "Yes! There is a place for them in our hearts and our churches!"

And that began a journey of Nepali women rescued from slavery in Mumbai to continue healing in their own country thanks to the welcome they received from local Nepali communities of faith.

Many girls and young women who have been rescued out of brothels and sexual slavery in India completed their education and have married and had children. They have completed their journeys to health and wholeness. In cultures that practice arranged marriages traditionally set up by birth parents, each of the marriages arranged by Project Rescue ministry leaders to wonderful young men of faith is a miracle of new life, a new "family," and the redeeming love of their heavenly Father.

The impossible happened in three major cities after years of spiritual battles. One by one, brothels within major red-light districts became available for purchase by Project Rescue to be used as outreach centers, becoming places of spiritual transformation and compassionate care. In fact, as these words are being written another former brothel has become a place of healing in the middle of darkness on another continent. Given the loss of income to organized crime that these transactions represent, these are miracles. As Jesus followers we believe God not only redeems people and makes them new; He also will ultimately redeem the earth on that day when He makes everything new. (See Revelation 21:5.) Each building and property redeemed for His life-changing purposes in the middle of great injustices is a down payment on that future day.

A little daughter in one of the red-light districts learned how to pray at a Project Rescue after-school program in the district. The more she learned about Jesus, the more her faith grew, and with childlike faith she believed every word He said. As this little girl, living in one of the world's darkest places, heard that Jesus prayed and healed people, she began to offer to pray for those in her community who were sick. One of those was a dying baby. This little girl prayed for the child, and miraculously the baby was healed! As this prostituted woman's daughter with great faith continued to pray for the sick, the people in the red-light district gave her a new name in their language. It meant "the girl who prays and God listens." It was another sign of God's kingdom on the earth!

In Europe, Africa, and South Asia, women and girls sold into prostitution have often been sacrificed to idols or had other demonic rituals performed over them. But hundreds of women and children have been delivered from this dark power and its destruction. They have become the redeemed daughters of God who are liberated and full of His empowering Spirit to love and worship God and bless those around them.

After the violence and trauma of years in sexual

slavery, victims typically have "hearts of stone," hearts hardened by rape and violence. Their once-tender hearts have become hardened by the loss of hope, hurt, violence, and experiencing the very worst of humanity. But God! The Hebrew prophet Ezekiel saw a day when God would turn "heart[s] of stone" into "heart[s] of flesh," a creative miracle we have seen thousands of times over in Project Rescue. (See Ezekiel 36:26.)

Heartbreaks and Mysteries

Over twenty-five years, our Project Rescue team has watched God perform amazing miracles and answers to prayer on behalf of sexually exploited persons. We have also experienced mysteries, the things that are so difficult to witness, experience, and understand. This is the hardest part of working with victims of sexual exploitation.

The most difficult days for Project Rescue leaders and team members are when women or children who have made so much hard-won progress to come out of the horrors of exploitation choose to go back to the men who exploited and brutalized them. Staff have worked 24/7 with the rescued women and children in aftercare homes, being there with them through tough days and nights of nightmares, terror, and chilling manifestations of dark power. Then at age eighteen, a girl chooses the next step in her life. Sadly, sometimes her "father" in the red-light district has been waiting for a chance to get her back into the business and will make unbelievable promises to entice her.

Staff do everything in their power to dissuade these girls, whom they have come to love like daughters, from making this disastrous decision. They encourage continuing education or vocational training toward their dreams, which Project Rescue scholarships will help fund. In most cases they are successful with God's help and much prayer, and young women decide to continue their healing journey. But some heart-breaking days, girls choose to go back into the very world from which they were rescued.

Sometimes young girls go back to visit their moms or family in home villages, and staff pray that they will return. Most often they do. But once in a while a girl is never seen again. There are rumors of tragedies, and sometimes staff members receive heartbreaking phone calls.

These heartbreaks are part and parcel of ministry to victims of sexual slavery. Despite prayer, professional skills, trauma counseling, and incredibly hard work, some women are enticed back and never heard from again. But we know that the God who is love, created them with dignity, and knows each girl by name will continue to reach out to them when they are out of our sight and influence. He still sees, still loves, and still does miracles to bring them back to Himself.

Every Project Rescue ministry leader, team member, intercessor, and supporter constantly challenges this dark world of horror to help women and children find hope and healing. Through tears of loss and tears of joy, across nations and oceans, our hope is not in Project Rescue but in Jesus, who came to earth, died on a cross, and was resurrected to life to set captives free and break chains of evil and bondage.

Chapter 9

WHAT WE PRAYED FOR

L IFE CHANGED DRASTICALLY when COVID-19 morphed into a global pandemic in March 2020. Planes stopped flying. Businesses were shuttered. Schools closed. Church services got suspended. Nations shut down. Unemployment skyrocketed. Previously unknown health officials appeared on television to tell us to "shelter in place."

We hoped the closures and suspensions would last a few weeks. But weeks stretched into months. Suddenly, we all had to do business differently. Church services went online, as did schools. Face-to-face meetings went virtual. Anxieties mounted. People feared losing their jobs, homes, and lives. There has been nothing like it in our lifetime; in fact, there has been nothing like it since the global flu pandemic of 1918.

Churches and ministries faced the prospect of dramatic declines in income. Project Rescue was no exception. We have monthly financial needs like every other ministry and deeply appreciate friends who make the ministry part of their monthly or annual giving. But as our leadership team prayed and talked about the challenges, we felt directed by the Lord *not* to ask our friends for money but to reach out to each one of them by phone to see how their families were doing and pray with them.

I (David) made hundreds of calls. The entire US team made calls. They spent the first two months of the COVID-19 pandemic staying in contact with the whole Project Rescue family and focusing on the daily struggles of friends and supporters.

The first wave of COVID-19 hit South Asia like a tsunami. Governments locked down the major cities in April and May. In South Asia, day laborers, who lack steady jobs but take work wherever they can find it, had nowhere to go but back to their home villages, often hundreds of miles away. Within hours of the lockdown order, the government closed all public transportation. Suddenly, the poorest of the poor, including women and children in the red-light districts, not only had to go home but also had to set out on foot without money or food. Thousands of people died every day. The pandemic had become a humanitarian crisis of monumental proportions.

We received a call from Devaraj. He said governments had closed red-light districts all over South Asia. All the brothels were closed.

Anyone who works with prostituted women and children prays for a day when places of exploitation will be shut down. We could hardly believe our ears.

In a matter of days, what we prayed for had come to pass in city after city. It seemed impossible.

Devaraj then added a sobering footnote: the women and children in the brothels were starving. If they could not work, they could not eat. Some brothel owners were throwing them into the street. They had nowhere to go. Could Project Rescue help?

Our response to the needs of the women and children trapped in sexual slavery has been the same since I (David) first walked through the city's red-light district twenty-five years ago: "Yes, we will help." So with brothels miraculously emptied, we prayed and called our team together. Then we reached out to friends around the world. We shared the need and the opportunity. Instead of rescuing a few young women and girls at a time over years, we had a window of opportunity to rescue hundreds, even thousands, within a matter of days.

It seemed like a dream. But God had done the impossible before. Project Rescue had seen God at work from the earliest day. We had seen the transformation of thousands of girls and young women. We had seen women and children healed of HIV/AIDS. Now God was doing it again.

The next few weeks were a blur of activity—long virtual conferences with team members across the Project Rescue network. Hundreds of phone calls to friends in the United States. The response was unlike anything we had seen. In six weeks we saw more financial contributions than in the previous year combined.

We sent the money out as fast as it came in. And God was faithful.

What Satan had meant for evil, God meant for good, and none of it would have been possible without the team of workers, prayer partners, and supporters God positioned for this moment of opportunity. Project Rescue has always been about the young women and girls devastated by the evil of sexual slavery. It came into being because of God's heart for the "least of these" (Matt. 25:40) and His incredible, unlimited compassion for the lost. Project Rescue has no other reason to exist. But now, suddenly, Project Rescue was seeing its greatest season of harvest in twenty-five years.

We were able to help people like Binita.

Changing "Fate"

At age sixteen, dreams of the future filled the mind of young Binita, who had just finished tenth grade. Smile beaming, Binita played on the swing outside her home, daydreaming until she heard familiar voices from inside her home.

Curious, she crept up to the house, peered in, and saw a familiar family friend. She eavesdropped. Her mother and uncle were discussing the tough times that had fallen upon their family since Binita's father abandoned them. With an older sister who had disappeared and two younger siblings still at home, Binita knew much of the responsibility would fall on her shoulders. After a few minutes her mother called for her to come in; she then told Binita that she had the opportunity to join a few girls traveling to the city to work in a factory.

The thought of leaving her humble village and moving to the city sounded intriguing and possibly even glamorous. Feeling the necessity to do her part, Binita agreed to go. Not long after, her auntie took her to the train station and handed Binita over to a "family" who would be traveling with her. She felt somewhat uneasy with them, yet when they offered Binita some food to eat, she graciously accepted, not realizing she was being drugged. Within minutes everything went dark.

Binita woke up coughing, finding herself surrounded by men in a strange room filled with smoke and loud music. Confused, she asked where she was but was met with cryptic answers in a language that sounded different from her own. Later, a woman grabbed her and told her she had been sold because her family needed the money. Horrified, Binita protested and said she had come to work in a factory. The woman glared at her and broke that illusion, saying, "Child, you *are* working in a factory—one that meets the needs of lusting men."

Refusing to do the work, Binita was deprived of food and water and kept locked in a dark, dingy room, just big enough to sleep and stand. The brothel owner was "breaking" her, but Binita was adamant that she was not going to do what they asked. Furious, the brothel owner did the unthinkable. He brought in a group of traffickers and pimps, telling them to drug and rape her until she submitted.

Ashamed, angry, broken, distraught, and humiliated, Binita soaked the floor of her small, dark room with tears, deciding that this must be her fate for reasons unknown to her. For years Binita worked in the red-light district until one day the police suddenly raided the brothel. Caught up in a flurry of events, Binita was taken to a government home and then sent back to her home village. Her return to the village was far from a warm reunion, and she quickly realized there was no place for her there. Her family was ostracized when the villagers discovered she was one of the "girls" who worked in the sex industry. Feeling alone and with nowhere else to go, Binita returned to the red-light district, telling herself, "This is my fate, so I must do it."

After living in the red-light district for a few months, she met a young man who befriended her and fell in love with her. He worked hard and over the course of a few months paid off her debt and married her. Soon after, she became pregnant and had a beautiful baby boy. Then the COVID-19 pandemic hit their family hard. Thankfully, it was during a Project Rescue relief outreach that she met the Project Rescue team and shared her story. Now working with Project Rescue and experiencing firsthand that "fate" can be changed, Binita helps other women like herself rewrite their destinies.

New Opportunities and
New Challenges

The explosion of opportunity created new challenges. We had been training people for ministry to the sexually exploited for more than twenty years. Most of that was face-to-face in classes, conferences, and seminars. Thousands of believers in the United States had been inspired and equipped to join the movement to minister grace and freedom to the oppressed. We knew it wasn't enough. Our virtual meetings gave us a hint of things to come. We began to think about training on a global scale through enhanced technology.

A six-course international training curriculum for ministry to the sexually exploited had been in the works with Continental Theological Seminary in Brussels for more than a year. Project Rescue leaders had planned to debut it in Brussels. COVID-19 altered that plan. Instead of one course in one place, the first course of Rescue & Restore was held simultaneously in ten countries and engaged many more students than we initially expected. It was now possible, for the first time in Project Rescue history, to train hundreds or even thousands of workers at the same time!

Next-Gen Leaders

A global pandemic challenged us to do more than we had ever done and believe God for even greater things. A different challenge that we had known was coming for a long time confronted the ministry. We (David and Beth) strongly believed the time had come to transition to a new generation of leadership. In 2016 our daughter Jennifer had joined the US Resource Office as administrator. We often say that Jennifer has her dad's energy and her mom's diplomacy. She had also grown up in the ministry. Our oldest daughter, Rebecca, was sixteen and Jennifer was twelve when we launched Project Rescue. The girls spent time in the homes in South Asia with girls their age who had been exploited, tortured, and raped. They heard the girls' stories and saw the trauma they suffered. Project Rescue became deeply personal to both Rebecca and Jennifer.

By the time Jennifer graduated high school, she was already thinking about where she might fit to give hope and a redeemed future to trafficked women and children. We never tried to influence either of our daughters to follow us in ministry.

Only God's call can sustain young people in any ministry, but especially in ministries directly challenging great evil.

As a nursing student, Jennifer met Mother Teresa and had been inspired by her care for the poor and dying. After college she became a registered nurse, eventually becoming the director of nursing for a skilled nursing/long-term-care facility. She understands the DNA of Project Rescue and had gained administrative skills during her years in nursing. After several years, the leadership of Project Rescue's board sensed that Jennifer was the right person to lead the ministry into a new season.

Jennifer's husband, Jonathan Barratt, is a young entrepreneur who went to high school with her before playing professional baseball for the Tampa Bay Rays organization. Jon advanced steadily through the minors until injuries ended his baseball career. Jon is blessed with an outstanding business mind. Today he leads the Project Rescue Foundation with an entrepreneurial spirit and strategic vision, which are critical to the support and sustainability of Project Rescue. Together, Jennifer and Jon are called, committed, and gifted to lead the Project Rescue ministry network into the future.

Founders play a unique role in any organization or ministry. They are motivated by a God-sized vision, possess boundless energy, and persevere in the face of challenges that would dishearten others. Second-generation leaders have a different calling—to build on the foundation, conserve the work, and think strategically about the future.

Project Rescue's decentralized structure has been a key to its success and sustainability. The birth of Project Rescue outreaches was "not the result of a grand strategy," as Project Rescue board member Kevin Donaldson has pointed out.[1] Every outreach began when one person walked through a red-light district in their city, saw the horror of sex trafficking, felt the heart of God for the enslaved, and began to share the love of Jesus with the victims. Face-to-face ministry to the sexually exploited has always generated the need for ministry centers, safe houses, and children's homes. Restoration followed.

We founded Project Rescue to support the ministry of a courageous pioneer and his team, who took hope to the women and children in the red-light district. We did not "launch" the outreach there. We supported the efforts of committed men and women on the front lines. That has been the pattern for twenty-five years. Every outreach was founded by a person with a vision God birthed in their hearts and with an embryonic network of support. In Europe, Project Rescue provided seed money for homes and training programs, raised awareness, and networked with other ministries.

Ultimately Project Rescue is about God's heart for the broken, His determination that none be lost, and His overflowing love that calls people to give their lives to "the least of these." In the United States, Project Rescue is known for its founders, but we speak pointedly to the issue: Project Rescue is not about David and Beth Grant; it is about the millions of children and young women trapped in the world of sexual slavery and the frontline ministers who are compelled by the love of Jesus to take hope to those in the world's greatest darkness.

When Project Rescue was born in a red-light district, it was about God's heart for His daughters and sons. It still is, and it will continue to be.

Chapter 10

TAKING ACTION

IN THE FACE of the entrenched evil of sex trafficking, it is reasonable to wonder what one person can do. Where do you start?

Former US representative Tony Hall of Dayton, Ohio, had just been appointed the chairman of the House Select Committee on Hunger. He was deeply concerned but had no idea where to begin. As he pondered and prayed about the problem, he concluded that he should start by traveling to Kolkata (formerly Calcutta) to visit an authority on the problem, Mother Teresa. Like many people who have visited Kolkata before and since, Hall was overwhelmed by what he saw. While in the city, he visited Mother Teresa and wanted to know what every person wonders when faced with staggering need: "The problems of the world are so vast. How can you possibly hope to solve them?"

The woman who had become the face of Christian

compassion to the world smiled gently and said, "You do the thing that's in front of you."[1]

That is the answer. No one person or group of persons can hope to bring an end to this life-destroying trade, but everyone can do what God puts in their hearts to do. Those who have been involved for years in efforts to set the captives free believe we are living in a unique moment. The local government leaders' reaching out to Project Rescue team members during the COVID-19 crisis suggests a window of opportunity that has never existed before. There is an unprecedented upsurge of compassion and Spirit-empowered activism around the world. That new spirit of activism can be seen in people of all ages and every demographic.

Joslyn was twelve years old when she read *Beyond the Soiled Curtain*, which describes Project Rescue's work. The suffering of young girls her age moved her heart, and she wanted to do something to help. She started cleaning houses, mowing lawns, and selling lemonade in her neighborhood. She saved all of her money for an entire summer. At the end of the summer, she gave $1,000 to Project Rescue.

You start where you are.

Brandy Crisafulli's husband, Chuck, comes from one of the oldest families in Brevard County, Florida. He grew up with civic and business leaders, including the mayor of their town, the sheriff, and county commissioners. Brandy and Chuck have leaned into every relationship to help these influencers understand the problem in *their* community and to seek support for a safe house for the young women trafficked in Florida's I-95 corridor.

You start where you are—regardless of your limitations.

A lot of people do not feel smart or gifted enough to make a difference. They could all take inspiration from Rich Dixon. Decades ago Rich was in an accident that left him paralyzed. One of the activities he enjoyed after his accident was hand cycling. His wife would ride a bike alongside him. They had an idea to host a bike ride with their church to raise money for Project Rescue. The couple held up a sign outside their church in Fort Collins, Colorado, that said, "Anybody want to go on a 500-mile bike ride?"

The first year, 2013, seven cyclists participated and raised $7,000. Their most recent ride not only attracted 150 local riders but also inspired thousands of riders nationwide and resulted in the Hope and Freedom Challenge, an initiative to raise funds and awareness for Project Rescue.

Pastors play a vital role in raising awareness and giving people opportunities to become involved in the cause of bringing freedom to the victims of sex trafficking. Mark Evans, a pastor from New Life Church in Trumbull, Connecticut, wanted to do more than pass the plate at their annual Christmas morning service. He challenged his congregation to go beyond their regular Christmas gift (the church has given this offering for over forty years) by bringing in any "old broken" pieces of jewelry, chains, rings that don't fit, single earrings, and so forth. Over the three weeks following Christmas, $50,000 in "scrap" gold was added to their offering of $50,000, making it the first year the church was able to give away $100,000.

Pastor Rod Loy may be one of the greatest change agents for Project Rescue. He and his church, First Assembly of God North Little Rock in Arkansas, have been walking with Project Rescue since the beginning. Under the direction of Pastor Alton Garrison, their church gave the $100,000 needed to purchase the first property in South Asia.

During the COVID-19 crisis, Pastor Rod helped mobilize churches and pastors across the country to partner with Project Rescue and launch the Forever Free campaign. His church gave its biggest offering to the ministry during COVID-19, with one of the most special gifts in that offering coming from nine-year-old Seth and six-year-old Becca, a brother and sister who sold most of their toys and brought their offering in a ziplock plastic bag.

Other churches reported that the offerings taken for Forever Free were the largest in their church's history. The mobilization led by Rod Loy resulted in the single greatest response in the history of the ministry and set Project Rescue on a new trajectory to walk through open doors in new cities and countries that once seemed impossible.

Over the past several years, Pastor Rod has joined two of his passions: seeing women and children in sexual slavery rescued and empowering women leaders to fulfill their God-given potential. What resulted from this connection was a generation of women lead pastors inspired and motivated to engage their churches with the work of Project Rescue. One of those pastors, Abbie Sawczak, has a beautiful story of uncommon faith and generosity.

Abbie serves as the lead pastor of New Culture Church in Madison, Wisconsin, and the director of Chi Alpha (an outreach to students at secular universities) at the University of Wisconsin–Madison. After attending a Project Rescue event, Abbie shared the vision with her team, and they knew they had to do something. They used their Christmas service to share about Project Rescue and encouraged the church to give the gift of hope by donating to Project Rescue. In addition to taking this one-time offering, the church started supporting Project Rescue monthly, a group of Chi Alpha students started making clay jewelry to raise funds and awareness, and another Chi Alpha group in Wisconsin was inspired to use their Valentine's Day event to raise money for Project Rescue.

You start where you are.

No one person or group of people has the capacity to take down sex trafficking. But when we allow God to birth His compassion in our hearts and offer ourselves as "broken bread," God takes what we give Him, and like the loaves and fishes, Jesus does more with what we put in His hands than we could ever have done ourselves.

WHERE DO YOU START?

Start with a prayer. Ask God to pour out His love for the broken into your heart. It is a simple prayer that can have big results. Bob Pierce visited Korea in the days after war had devastated the Korean peninsula, resulting in the deaths of more than a million people and poverty and deprivation throughout the country. More than one million children were orphaned. Disease and hunger were everywhere. Bob wrote a prayer that he carried in his Bible the rest of his life: "Let my heart be broken with the things that break the heart of God." God's answer to that prayer was World Vision and Samaritan's Purse.[2]

Ask God for divine appointments. Project Rescue has been characterized by divine appointments in every place where team members have gone. It may have started with giving a trafficked woman a flower in Antwerp or a walk down a street in a red-light district. Be assured that God does not love the women and men who work in Project Rescue any more than He loves you. You might try getting up tomorrow morning and saying, "Jesus, what are You and I doing today?" Then let Him make it happen.

Let God supply your needs. A lot of people talk themselves out of doing anything because they are waiting for the resources. God's name is Jehovah

Jireh—He is the God who sees and provides. (See Genesis 22:14, AMP.) The Bible is the story of people who responded to God's voice by venturing out and giving Him the opportunity to live up to His name. A Hebrew sage said, "Cast your bread upon the waters, for you will find it after many days" (Eccles. 11:1, NKJV). The key to divine provision is simple: take what you have and put it out there, then give God a chance to prove Himself great. If you wait until you have the "right" opportunity or the resources you need, you will never do anything.

DON'T GO IT ALONE

This last word of counsel may be the most important. Don't try to be a superhero. You are not wired for it. No one is. When Jesus sent His first followers out to take on the dark kingdom by announcing the coming of His kingdom, healing the sick, and casting out demons, He sent them out two by two. That tells us everyone needs support and encouragement.

There is nothing to stop you from going it alone, but if you do you are certain to become discouraged and defeated. And there will not be anyone there to help you.

If you give Him a chance, you can be sure that God will either connect you to an existing ministry like Project Rescue or He will bring people alongside you to help. And by the way, we are here to help you. Connect by way of our website. Send us an email.

Start where you are! Join the global effort to bring freedom to the women and children held in sexual slavery.

ACKNOWLEDGMENTS

FROM HORROR TO HOPE would not have been possible without the help of dozens of Project Rescue team members whose faithful service to Christ and the most vulnerable has been at the heart of this ministry for a quarter century. Their dedication, sacrifice, and deep insight into the plight of victims of sex trafficking made this book possible.

First and foremost, we want to thank the ministry leaders to whom this book is dedicated. Their selfless dedication to rescuing and restoring the victims of sex trafficking has provided the inspiration for much of what we do. They took time out of often impossible schedules for interviews and provided the stories on which this book is based. Their comments and suggestions have helped us get the story right. The stories in this book are their stories.

We also want to thank the team members who have read the manuscript and added their own perspectives to the story. Special appreciation goes to Kellie Dennis, who arranged interviews, tirelessly researched statistics, and worked with us on the technical editing.

Scores of colleagues, too numerous to name, have been our partners in the great work of bringing the light of God's presence to some of the darkest corners of the earth. We are indebted to them for their counsel and support.

We also want to thank the hundreds of churches, pastors, and friends who have sown prayers and finances into our ministry, in some cases for decades. Because of you we have always been "covered," especially in moments of crisis and trial. We want to express special appreciation to our dear friends Rod Loy and Mark Lehmann and the churches they lead, First Assembly of God North Little Rock in Arkansas and Cornerstone Church in Bowie, Maryland.

We also want to thank our friend Gary Kellner for his extensive, excellent work with us on this project and for his heart for the ministry of Project Rescue.

Finally, we want to thank you for taking the time to read *From Horror to Hope*. It is our prayer that God will use it to challenge you to extend His ministry of rescue and restoration to the broken in your world.

We celebrate twenty-five years of God's faithfulness and every woman and child who has been liberated from this horror to hope. And we commit ourselves to fight this battle for victims of sexual slavery together for years to come.

IN STEP WITH THE SPIRIT[1]

Authentic Pentecostal Leadership for
Disorienting Times

By Beth Grant

I N SPRING 2020, when COVID-19 was just beginning to spread across the U.S., Assemblies of God
World Missions Executive Director Greg Mundis
was suddenly hospitalized with the virus and fighting
for his life. Because my husband, David, and I had
worked with him that same week, we found ourselves
in quarantine with lots of time to intercede for Greg
and other friends.

During that time, I started saying something at the
end of phone calls with family and friends that I'd
never said in my life: "Stay safe!"

That was my heart. But I soon became uncomfortable with the words as I said them. A still, small voice
I've come to know challenged me: "Beth, never in your
life have I called you to the priority of staying safe.

I've always called you to stay ready...ready to hear My voice, ready to obey, ready to discern what I am doing and to move with Me. Yes, be wise. But I'm calling you first to stay ready. Don't miss now what I'm going to do in this storm!"

David and I serve as co-directors of Project Rescue, an Assemblies of God outreach to victims of sexual slavery. I shared this message with our leadership team in the U.S. and ministry leaders in [South Asia] and Europe. Together, they affirmed this was a word from the Lord. "Stay ready!" became our spiritual call to arms.

Within weeks—while many leaders were still in quarantine, in lockdown, or fighting COVID-19—we received amazing news. Red-light districts in Europe and [South Asia] shut down, and shut out tourists seeking illicit sex. Pimps and brothel owners turned out prostituted women and their children because it was no longer profitable to keep them.

For the first time in the 24-year history of Project Rescue, thousands of enslaved women and children had a chance to leave their horrific situation and receive help and freedom through our ministry.

But someone had to move quickly to get them to safety. Because God had spoken and prepared us by His Spirit, ministry leaders were ready to take personal risks and do exactly what God had called them to do. In the middle of a global storm, God was opening prison doors and turning hearts toward Jesus.

Changing Times

Before the pandemic, U.S. churches had enjoyed a long period of relative stability. Community life was fairly predictable, and the ability to gather for church was a given.

Amid this comfortable environment, many ministers adopted secular business models of leadership. With strategic planning and a well-trained leadership team, success seemed inevitable. But over time, secular leadership models can move us away from reliance on the Holy Spirit.

Then came the crises of 2020–21. Assumptions about church schedules, planning, events, missions, and travel collided with shocking new realities. And Pentecostal leaders awakened to the need for a course correction.

The context of leadership has changed dramatically—both inside and outside the Church. Over the past year, the world has witnessed the inadequacy of leadership models that depend solely on human systems. We've seen the limitations of economic, scientific, political and psychological knowledge. The pandemic, racial tensions, political chaos, and natural disasters have confounded policymakers and pundits and exposed our frailty and fallibility.

The needs within the community of faith have changed as well. Like everyone else, Christians are facing the raw uncertainties of life, the loss of loved ones, family tensions, and unemployment. People everywhere are dealing with overwhelming challenges, fear and trauma.

Our sense of normalcy within the Church is gone. Ministries have adapted quickly to navigate realities they never could have anticipated. How many church leaders had a strategy for ministering to believers in a masked, socially distanced setting, or for suddenly moving all services and group meetings online?

Privately, stress has mounted and weaknesses have surfaced. When leaders are on the platform and systems are functioning well, personal vulnerabilities are easier to ignore.

But when circumstances strip away our safe and familiar routines, we come face-to-face with our own humanity—and our urgent need for God's empowering presence. Many veteran pastors and missionaries have looked in the mirror and realized their need to check back in to the spiritual formation journey.

The world has shifted under our feet, and it will continue to change. We can't predict what our cities, our nation, or our world will face in six months—much less five years. For many of us, the future seems more unknowable than ever before.

Pentecostal church and ministry leaders today are acutely aware of their need for the Holy Spirit. We are desperate for the Spirit's guidance. Only God knows the future. He can lead us supernaturally by His Spirit, and reaffirm His unshakable truth and lordship.

For people of the Spirit, this is the best of times to lean into the Spirit. His presence, His power, His guidance, and His gifts are freely available to empower us in every season.

Spirit-Led Ministry

A respected veteran missionary was taking a graduate course, "Developing a Pentecostal Theology of Leadership." On the last day of class, he admitted he had experienced an "Aha!" moment. The missionary was a student of leadership and had developed a personal leadership model and vision statement. But it had never crossed his mind that his Pentecostal theology should shape his model and practice of leadership.

He's probably not alone. So, what *is* authentic Pentecostal leadership? And how should our identity as Spirit-filled believers affect our identities as leaders?

Authentic Pentecostal leaders rely on the fulness of the Spirit for preaching and serving (Acts 1:8). God-given spiritual gifts accompany their ministry (1 Corinthians 12:7–11; Galatians 5:22).

Those who follow Pentecostal leaders should also hunger for and experience the fulness of God's Spirit, learn to serve others by the empowerment of the Spirit, and minister in the Kingdom through spiritual gifts.

Distinguishing marks of authentic Pentecostal leadership include the following:

God's presence. Authentic Pentecostal leaders are Spirit-filled and anointed for ministry by the Spirit day by day. They seek God passionately and welcome His unmistakable presence with them. Leaders approach each day with readiness to hear God's voice, sense His guidance, and obey Him in faith. Others know them as people who live and walk in God's presence.

Supernatural discernment. Many Christian leaders know intellectually through God's Word and His promises that He is still at work in the world. But authentic Pentecostal leaders have affirmation of that confidence because they spiritually discern God at work—even in the middle of crises, suffering and storms.

Leaders listen for His voice, and they sense, discern, and respond to His Spirit. In addition to an intellectual engagement with a Pentecostal theology of the Spirit, leaders experientially engage their theology of the Spirit in the way they minister, serve in leadership, and fulfill God's call—whatever their context.

Dynamic integration. Because they believe it's possible and desirable to walk in the Spirit with sensitivity daily, authentic Pentecostal leaders are less likely to limit participation in the spiritual gifts to prescribed days, times and spaces.

The New Testament provides accounts of the Holy Spirit leading, anointing, and ministering to and through Jesus' disciples on the streets, in homes, in prison, on a ship, on the road, and even while running alongside a chariot. The Spirit did not restrict His work to traditionally sacred places.

Where God's people went full of the Spirit, the Spirit of the Lord worked dynamically through them.

Unusual seasons of spiritual challenge and

opportunity are strategic times for leaders to welcome Scripture-informed participation in all God-given gifts (1 Corinthians 12:1–11) so that the Church may be strong and well-equipped for God's mission.

When the epic battle with evil goes to a new level, picky spiritual appetites do not serve leaders, the church, individual believers, or the mission well. Pentecostal church leaders have a responsibility to teach believers about spiritual gifts and provide opportunities for them to seek and receive the fullness of the Spirit.

The Church of 2021 needs all the gifts God has provided for His people by His Spirit. He calls us not just to survive times of suffering; God desires to give us strength and empowerment for life-changing transformational ministry in the midst of difficulties.

Countercultural courage. Famed missiologist Lesslie Newbigin asked, "From whence comes the voice that can challenge this culture on its own terms, a voice that speaks its own language and yet confronts it with the authentic figure of the crucified and living Christ so that it is stopped in its tracks and turned back from the way of death?"

Authentic Pentecostal leaders courageously challenge cultural and religious norms that are in conflict with God's Word and the work of the Spirit.

In Acts 10, it was the disarming work of the Holy Spirit that gave Peter a vision to take the gospel beyond the Jews to the Gentiles—and to see people through God's eyes rather than cultural and religious eyes.

The reality that Jesus offered salvation to all people confronted Peter's personal belief system. But when God confronted him through a vision, Peter received correction and was willing to pivot immediately and become a voice of God's redemptive plan for the Gentiles.

It still takes Spirit-guided courage to communicate truth and challenge the cultural, political and religious status quo of the day in ways that lead listeners to the living Christ.

Prophetic discernment. Authentic Pentecostal leaders understand the times in which they live. They can discern truth from lies of the enemy, and good from evil. Paul talks about distinguishing between spirits—knowing what's of God and what's from Satan.

Hebrews 5:11–14 warns believers against apostasy and laments the spiritual immaturity of some. The author describes mature believers as those who have "trained themselves to distinguish good from evil" (verse 14).

I was born into a Pentecostal church and have observed people of the Spirit throughout my life. I believe one of the most undervalued and underutilized but needed gifts of the Spirit in today's world is spiritual discernment, integrated with wisdom and knowledge.

Supernatural discernment is necessary for church leaders and parishioners as many false teachers distort God's truth and seek to deceive. Articulate, charismatic leaders and celebrities speak words that sound religious, Christian and biblical. It takes spiritual discernment to determine the spirit behind the words. Is it of God? Satan himself quotes God's Word insidiously to achieve his own destructive ends (Matthew 4:5–6).

In Acts 5, Luke shares an account of Peter operating in the gifts of discernment and knowledge after Pentecost. Ananias and his wife, Sapphira, came to Peter publicly to present an offering. Tragically, they misrepresented their generosity before God, Peter and the church.

Peter's stunning revelation of this couple's deception and their subsequent deaths is one of the most sobering moments in the New Testament church. After witnessing Peter's discernment in that moment, it would have been hard to doubt his authentic, Spirit-empowered leadership.

Spiritual authority. Authentic Pentecostal leaders appropriate the authority Jesus delegated in Matthew 28:18–20. Thus, the kingdom of darkness and its evil manifestations do not intimidate them. Under the anointing of the Spirit, they stand with courage and lean into the battle in His authority when facing spiritual opposition. Leaders exercise authority not to advance their own interests, but to fulfill Christ's redemptive mission on earth.

The reality of darkness and our desperation to walk in authentic spiritual authority became personal when I first went into the red-light districts of [South Asia] to minister. For the first time in my life, I entered a place so evil, violent and demonic the darkness was palpable and intimidating.

I soon realized there wasn't enough of God's power at work in me to take authority over the power of Satan that enslaves women and children. I began to live desperately and dependently on a powerful, fresh anointing of His Spirit as I battled the forces of hell itself.

When encountering Satan's dark power, our official positions, ministerial credentials, academic degrees, and charismatic personalities are irrelevant. There was a reason Jesus sent His followers to the Upper Room 2,000 years ago to wait for Pentecost before they headed out to minister. Jesus knew His Great Commission mandate was absolutely impossible to accomplish without His accompanying supernatural power and authority.

Paul's words to the Ephesians make our source of power clear and leave no doubt about our enemy:

> Finally, be strong in the Lord and in his mighty power. Put on the full armor of God, so that you can take your stand against the devil's schemes. For our struggle is not against flesh and blood, but against the rulers, against the authorities, against the powers of this dark world and against the spiritual forces of evil in the heavenly realms.
>
> —EPHESIANS 6:10–12

Spiritual Alignment

How do we align ourselves toward more authentically Pentecostal leadership?

First, be intentional about practicing God's presence each day. When we daily walk with an awareness of His presence, we will hear and know God's voice well. People of God's presence more readily recognize any presence or power that is not of God—wherever they are, whether in sacred or secular places.

Pentecostal leaders also have the privilege of mentoring those they lead to practice God's presence every day. These leaders invest in helping others become more genuinely engaged with God's Spirit daily and less vulnerable to deception and the influence of dark spiritual power (1 John 4:1–3).

Second, intentionally steward your voice. Whatever, wherever your platform, don't underestimate what God can do. Prayerfully seek Him for Spirit-defined and anointed words. Whether preaching, communicating through a podcast or blog, leading a small group, participating in a prison ministry, attending a board meeting, or talking with a friend over coffee, humbly bring God's presence and anointing with you.

The Spirit of the Lord speaking truth through us disarms hearts, minds and spirits to convict of sin, save, heal, bring words of wisdom, and deliver from bondage.

Church leaders cannot assume their message is changing hearts and minds. Consider how few voices people heard a decade ago compared to how many voices they hear today. Through digital tools, especially social media, millions of people now have platforms and listeners.

Why should people listen to your voice or to mine? But when we speak with God's authority, anointing, and grace, His truth can cut through the auditory overload and touch souls with personal precision. That's a work of the Spirit.

Third, prayerfully ask and discern what God is doing in this prophetic day. In peaceful seasons and in troubled times, He is at work in the world. The question isn't just what God is up to, but also how we can align our hearts, strategies and resources with His plans. How can we inspire those we serve to step into what God is doing in our world, with faith and courage rather than fear?

God, by His Spirit, can give us eyes to understand the times, as the sons of Issachar did in 1 Chronicles 12:32. We need spiritual leaders who have their finger on the pulse of our times and understand its significance to the work of the Kingdom.

Fourth, check your personal thoughts, motivations and emotions. We are living in a time of disturbing volatility, political anger, explosive words, and unbridled actions.

In such an environment, ministry leaders need to check their hearts before communicating on any platform. Is the passion we feel the Holy Spirit's anointing to communicate God's message? Or is it simply the stirring of our own opinions and emotions—a natural human response to what is happening around us?

Just because we are Pentecostal leaders does not mean all passion we feel is of God.

At all times, wise Pentecostal leaders prayerfully guard their thoughts, attitudes, motivations and emotions. Discern prayerfully, speak wisely, and use silence strategically, as Jesus did, in ways that consistently honor our Heavenly Father.

Fifth, be honest with those you lead when you miss it. Recently, a well-known Christian leader made a public apology. He had made some supposedly prophetic predictions that turned out to be false. So, using the same platform from which he had delivered the erroneous message, the leader humbly acknowledged he had been wrong. He took responsibility for his words as a leader and ended his apology with reassuring faith and hope in God, whose Word never fails.

God alone remains ever-faithful, all-knowing, and all-powerful. The future ultimately rests in His hands alone.

Pentecostal leaders are redeemed, called...and human. Participating with God and the work of the Holy Spirit in mission is not an exact science. It requires humility and integrity. The good news is that the more leaders seek to follow the Spirit's lead and practice simple obedience, the more readily they can discern and obey.

Finally, rethink your plans. Several years ago, I

looked at our nonstop travel and ministry schedule in the U.S. and overseas and felt God's conviction.

I sensed the Lord saying, "Beth, if I bring the unplanned person or open door to you, is there even time in your schedule for Me to work? Are you willing to make room for Me to do the unexpected and miraculous by My Spirit?"

This is a profound—and uncomfortable—question. Is there space in our personal planner and church calendar for God to move in fresh ways during this season? Or are church and ministry schedules so packed with the good and predictable there is little time for God to move freely by His Spirit and do the great and unpredictable? Are we allowing room for the people we serve to cry out to God and respond to the fresh wind of the Spirit that is blowing?

Yes, plan well. But also consider how you can simplify, scale back, and build in margin so you can adapt quickly to follow the Spirit's lead.

I believe God is raising up Spirit-empowered pioneers for a new season of harvest. He may call us to be among them—or to mentor young people who will break new ground in the final hours before Jesus returns.

Can we release some things we've always done to embrace the things God loves to do and has promised to do into the future? The Spirit of the Lord is moving! Let's make margin for miracles.

READY AND IN STEP

For six months in 2020, Project Rescue ministry teams had God-opened doors to minister to more than 1,000 prostituted women and their children.

Assemblies of God pastors and churches in the U.S. heard about the opportunities and stepped up, too. It was deeply moving to see how quickly and generously they gave in the middle of their own challenging days. As a result, Project Rescue had resources in hand to respond and share Christ's love and compassion with the sexually exploited during an extraordinary window of time.

Recently, a brothel in a major red-light district became available for us to buy and turn into a ministry center. Soon, women and children in slavery on those infamous dark streets will meet Jesus in our new facility, find freedom from the power of evil, and learn what it means to live as redeemed, Spirit-filled people of God.

The apostle Paul's words to the Galatian church are fitting for Pentecostal leaders today: "Since we live by the Spirit, let us keep in step with the Spirit" (Galatians 5:25).

May we stay ready and in step with Him during this significant season for our Father's glory and the fulfillment of His great mission.

RECOMMENDED READING

Project Rescue

Beyond the Soiled Curtain: Project Rescue's Fight for the Victims of the Sex-Slave Industry by David and Beth Grant

Sex Trafficking

Hands That Heal: International Curriculum to Train Caregivers of Trafficking Survivors edited by Beth Grant and Cindy Lopez Hudlin

Trafficking in Persons Report by the US Department of State

Ending Human Trafficking: A Handbook of Strategies for the Church Today by Shayne Moore, Sandra Morgan, and Kimberly McOwen Yim

Stopping the Traffick: A Christian Response to Sexual Exploitation and Trafficking edited by Glenn Miles and Christa Foster Crawford

Leaving Silence: Sexualized Violence, the Bible, and Standing With Survivors by Susannah Larry and Kat Armas

Walk Into Freedom: Christian Outreach to People Involved in Commercial Sexual Exploitation by Ruth H. Robb and Marion L. S. Carson

COMPASSION MINISTRY

Courageous Compassion: Confronting Social Injustice God's Way by Beth Grant

Healing the Wounds of Trauma: How the Church Can Help, Expanded Edition 2016 by Harriet Hill, Margaret Hill, Richard Baggé, and Pat Miersma (available in multiple languages)

From the Roots Up: A Closer Look at Compassion and Justice in Missions by JoAnn Butrin

Pentecostals and the Poor: Reflections From the Indian Context by Ivan Satyavrata

Good News About Injustice: A Witness of Courage in a Hurting World by Gary A. Haugen

NOTES

Chapter 2

1. Norman Grubb, *C. T. Studd: Cricketer & Pioneer* (Fort Washington, PA: CLC Publications, 1933, 2008), 145.

Chapter 3

1. Rod Loy, phone call with the authors, December 22, 2021.

Chapter 4

1. Rod Loy, phone call with the authors.
2. John Newton, "Amazing Grace," Hymnal.net, accessed April 4, 2022, https://www.hymnal.net/en/hymn/h/313.

Chapter 5

1. John C. Maxwell, *The 17 Indisputable Laws of Teamwork* (New York: HarperCollins, 2001).
2. Ivan Satyavrata, video call with the authors, January 18, 2022.

Chapter 6

1. Paul Trementozzi, conversation with the authors, February 20, 2018.
2. Fiona Bellshaw, video call with the authors, January 11, 2022.
3. Tim Wegner, conversation with the authors, October 2017.

Chapter 7

1. Henri Nouwen, *Bread for the Journey* (New York: Harper One, 2006), 166.

CHAPTER 9

1. Kevin Donaldson, video call with the authors, January 25, 2022.

CHAPTER 10

1. Tony Hall with Tom Price, *Changing the Face of Hunger* (Nashville: Thomas Nelson, 2006), 36.
2. Rich Stearns, "Blessed by a Broken Heart," World Vision, August 28, 2017, https://www.worldvision.org/hunger-news-stories/blessed-broken-heart.

APPENDIX A

1. Beth Grant, "In Step With the Spirit," *Influence*, April–June 2021, https://influencemagazine.com/en/issues/in-step-with-the-spirit, 39–46. Reprinted with permission. Quote by Lesslie Newbigin is from Lesslie Newbigin, *Foolishness to the Greeks* (Grand Rapids, MI: Wm. B. Eerdmans Publishing Co., 1986).

CONTACT US

PROJECT
RESCUE

www.projectrescue.com
info@projectrescue.com
417-833-5564

Project Rescue
PO Box 922
Springfield, MO 65801